To Down
With best wishes

Edward D. Heyer

9/16/90

Why Good Parents
Have Bad Kids

Why Good Parents Have Bad Kids

How to Make Sure That Your Child Grows Up Right

E. KENT HAYES

Doubleday

NEW YORK   LONDON   TORONTO   SYDNEY   AUCKLAND

Published by Doubleday, a division of Bantam Doubleday Dell Publishing Group, Inc., 666 Fifth Avenue, New York, New York 10103.

DOUBLEDAY and the portrayal of an anchor with a dolphin are trademarks of Doubleday, a division of Bantam Doubleday Dell Publishing Group, Inc.

Library of Congress Cataloging-in-Publication Data

Hayes, E. Kent.
Why good parents have bad kids : how to make sure that your child grows up right / E. Kent Hayes. — 1st ed.
    p. cm.
  1. Parenting.   2. Child rearing.   I. Title.
HQ755.8.H4   1989   88-18738
649'.1—dc19

This book is dedicated to a group of very special people called family-care parents. From them I have learned of the healing power of quality parenting. Within the homes of people like Ed and Ilene Fazzone, Florence and Kenneth Preston, David and Elena Canez, Joseph and Dziko Emu, and Pat and Phil McPhail, I have watched miracles take place.

Acknowledgments

This book turned out to be a group project and would never have seen the light of day without the superb and sensitive editing skills of my son Michael; the know-how-to-do-everything skills of my colleague Shirley Sloan; the selfless cover of job responsibilities by my partner, Dr. Alex Lazzarino; and the ever-present love and support of my beautiful wife, Ginger.

Contents

Author's Note

In an effort to safeguard the privacy of the children and family-care parents I have worked with, I have made multiple alterations of detail in every one of the case histories given in this book. Although each story is based upon real events, I have in every case changed names, disguised identifying characteristics, and, in some cases, created composite characters to avoid identification. Since what I have written applies equally to children of either sex, I have alternated the use of he and she by chapter.

Why Good Parents
Have Bad Kids

Introduction

John and Pamela Winston sat at the edge of the straight-back chairs looking at each other self-consciously and ignoring the other people in the waiting room. Pamela twisted a handkerchief in her hands while John smoked one cigarette after another. He thought he had completely rid himself of the habit, but the telephone call in the middle of the night three months earlier had left him feeling weak and dependent. John looked at Pamela and silently vowed to take her on a long vacation—perhaps that trip to China she had talked about before the trouble started. A nervous tic danced erratically beneath the skin of her left cheek, and the beautiful blue eyes were cradled in dark rings. John leaned forward and kissed her gently on the mouth. For a moment she looked shocked, but then she placed her head on his shoulder and cried.

John Winston is vice president in charge of foreign investments at a large bank in a midsized city in the western United States. He is on the board of directors of the university from which he graduated with honors, and contributes generously in time and money to community social concerns. Pamela Winston could be labeled a professional volunteer. She is on the boards of three charities and is president of her sorority chapter. Their only child, Robert, is a criminal and is now a convict serving ten to twenty years at the state penitentiary. Two days after his twentieth birthday, he was arrested for the armed robbery of a liquor store six blocks from his parents' home.

The Winstons refused to look at the other people in the prison waiting room because they are embarrassed and ashamed. If they could resurrect some honest prejudice, they would admit to feeling out of place and superior to those who spawn criminals. What they are about to discover is that other people like themselves are facing almost identical problems.

John and Pamela are learning the hard way about a growing sociological phenomenon and are being exposed to one of America's best-kept secrets. Today's prison population is a cross section of every religion, creed, race, and social class. Children raised in middle- and upper-income homes are no longer immune to the indignities of the prison environment. The belief that all prisoners are poverty stricken and ignorant is a twentieth-century wives' tale. Other well-meaning mothers and fathers who own homes on treelined streets in communities all over the United States are suffering as their children struggle to maintain sanity in mental hospitals, or praying to understand why their loved one chose suicide rather than continue the struggle.

The Institute of Medicine's Division of Mental Health and Behavioral Medicine reported in 1985 that an estimated eight to ten million children suffer from emotional disorders or experience developmental difficulties.

For the past twenty-five years, as I have worked with the children of disrupted families, I have watched this cancer spread into the homes of that segment of our society which has traditionally represented the backbone of our social order. Through daily contact, observation, and research, I have made some startling discoveries, but one essential factor remains constant: Parental neglect is the primary force promoting the evolution of today's disturbed child.

At one point, the professionals who study criminal behavior concluded that the discarded waifs who are turned loose in the world without supervision or love were obvious candidates for a life of crime. One of the key ingredients in this destructive mixture was poverty. Poverty breeds depression, anxiety, and, eventually, a desperation that often culminates in neglect. Neglect is the key word. If this is true, what could be the causative agent for this new breed of upper-class miscreants? Let me say it again: *Parental neglect* continues to be the primary force promoting the evolution of today's criminal.

There is little evidence that certain "special" babies exit

the womb destined for a life of crime. Neither is crime a profession of choice. It is not on the list of optional lectures during the career-day presentations in high school. Our young people do not ponder vocations and conclude that crime is the most logical choice.

The fact is that criminals are formed by their environment. But John and Pamela Winston would, like most of us who perceive ourselves to be good and caring parents, seriously resent this accusation. It would be very difficult for them to remember an incident while they were raising their son, Robert, when they were neglectful or even uncaring. What the Winstons do not know is that the traditional demands of parenting have changed radically. The rules are different, and our children are facing emotional and moral hurdles that did not exist when our generation was growing up. Today's mothers and fathers must learn a new set of skills if they expect to arm their offspring with the tools necessary to function in a world ripe with potential, but filled with pitfalls that were unknown twenty years ago.

Perhaps it's unfair to imply that most of us do, in fact, neglect our children. But keep in mind that the type of neglect I am talking about *can* and *does* occur in your home. It would be impossible to count the number of bright, conscientious people who have wept on my shoulder as their children were handcuffed and taken off to jail. They are dumbfounded when they comprehend what has happened to them, and their responses are basically the same: "I was a good parent. I gave him everything he needed. We loved him. People in our family don't go to prison. How could this be?"

The shock and disbelief are matched only by the shame

and, eventually, the guilt. They conclude that they have done something wrong, but they are also honest when they say that they do not know what it is they have done. As I analyze these tragedies and guide families through the wrenching process of self-evaluation, I begin to see certain patterns of behavior. The formula for destruction begins to emerge, and in almost every situation I can tell them why their child no longer perceives society's rules to apply to his or her own life.

Analyzing or understanding the motives and behavior of parents has not always been my top priority. But I remember well the day I had the revelation that changed all that. The event was not dramatic, and the others present would not have noticed anything remarkable about the occasion.

In August 1963, I was director of court services in the juvenile court of a Midwestern city. It was a hot Friday afternoon, and we had finally reached the last case on the long docket. The white-faced clock that had long since turned yellow, just above the judge's head, said it was five thirty-five, but it was consistently ten minutes slow. Everything in the old courthouse was either broken or slow.

The judge sat high on a carved wood dais behind a large desk, and the family, consisting of a small, haggard mother, an eleven-year-old son, and a runny-nosed baby, huddled behind a conference table in front of the dais. The boy's probation officer sat at the end of their table and the guardian ad litem (the court-appointed attorney) sat beside them. I attended most of the hearings, but participated only when one of my probation officers needed help or screwed up. On that particular occasion I was sitting in the first row of spectator seats, and because juvenile hearings are confidential, I was the only person behind the low wooden railing. Because I sat alone, out of the direct line of fire, I was able to maintain a certain objectivity. If it hadn't been for the mother's outburst, I would have used my detached position to tune out and start daydreaming about the weekend that was already forty-five minutes late in beginning.

The judge asked Billy's mother why she could not control her son. He was eleven years old and had been involved in seven violations that had required police intervention. She shook her head and rocked back and forth. When he asked the question again, she began to moan. The moan grew slowly, like the revving up of a siren, until it was a shriek. Her baby began to cry, and Billy put his arm around his mother's shoulder in a helpless attempt to comfort her. The judge came down from the dais, the probation officer took the baby, the mother settled down, and the hearing proceeded. I walked to the table to pick up the case file and returned to my seat. It was a typical case; there was nothing within the thick folder that surprised me.

Typical in this context meant that Billy first came to the court at the age of two on a neglect petition. His father had beaten both him and his mother. Billy suffered two broken bones, multiple bruises and lacerations, and had gone into shock before his mother could get him to the hospital. The father was charged with child abuse and left town, never to return. The mother broke down six months later and was admitted to the state mental hospital. During her nine-month stay there, Billy was shuttled between three foster homes. There were two other neglect petitions related to the mother's inability to cope.

It was typical. If someone had sat next to me in the courtroom on that hot August afternoon and asked what the case was about, I would have shrugged and said, "Typical stuff." I don't remember how it ended, but I do remember Billy's face and the bright, confused, compassionate eyes. I remember thinking when I got in my car to go home that Billy was now lost. It was over. Unless a miracle occurred, Billy would become a statistic. Billy was being sucked into a whirlpool of events that lead to prison, a state hospital, or a violent death. And we all sat back and watched complacently as it happened over and over to all the Billys that stumbled through our courtroom. It had become so routine that we simply accepted the inevitable, without maintaining hope. Hope was for the newcomers, the novices just out of school, with their pink cheeks and useless knowledge. It was chic to be hardened and embittered. I realized years later that our calloused attitude was a cover for the frustration associated with constant failure.

The revelation. I started this thought by saying I had a revelation on that day twenty-five years ago. The revelation was not about the inevitable progression from neglect to delinquency, which was one element that made the case typical. The revelation was not the notion that neglect was the disease and that delinquency, crime, and mental illness were simply the symptoms, though this was equally true. The revelation, that fateful day, was simply that hundreds of thousands of parents were destroying their kids' futures because they did not know how to parent, or for some other reason, often beyond their control, could not parent. The only real preventive or cure for these children was good parenting.

I saw rich kids, poor kids, and middle-class kids falling

into the same traps. I saw caring but ineffectual parents begging for help, but we spent most of our time trying to treat or punish their kids.

The revelation was that society has spent hundreds of years vacillating between the treatment and punishment theories of care. The punishment group says that the little bastards are bad, and if you put them in kiddy prisons, where they will be lonely and lost and hurt, they will never again violate the law for fear of returning to the awful place. The treatment people say no, they are not bad, they are sick, and given the right kind of psychiatric treatment they will get well. What I realized that Friday afternoon was that Billy needed the same things that my own children needed in the process of growing up. Billy needed parenting. Billy was a bright, normal kid from an abnormal environment. If I had grown up in his home, I, too, would be confused and angry.

I spent most of that night walking up and down the sidewalk in front of my home thinking there had to be a way to parent these children. From that point on I have never stopped thinking about parenting and its impact on our offspring.

From the juvenile court I became the superintendent of a reform school, where we incarcerated 365 boys from six to nineteen years of age. After a thorough evaluation of the school population, we discovered that 68 percent of the boys were neglected children; children in need of parenting, not barbed fences, locked steel doors, or shaved heads. I stood by and helplessly watched children deteriorate before my eyes.

My experience in the reform school was the final blow that provided the motivation to begin the search. The seed that was planted on that summer afternoon in 1963 when I looked into Billy's bright, confused eyes took root. I left the institution and began to develop a new concept of care for delinquent, neglected children.

Today, we have family-care homes in six states and the District of Columbia where children are growing up to be healthy, contributing members of society. A place where Billy could live just like any other kid on the block. The project that I am presently working on with my partner, Dr. Alex Lazzarino, is called the Menninger Youth Program and is located at the world famous Menninger Clinic. It is now a nationally recognized concept of care. From the beginning we have referred to the program as CHARLEE, an acronym for Children Have All Rights: Legal, Educational, Emotional. The CHARLEE model is not based on clinical treatment or on institutionalized correction, but rather on restoring—and in some cases providing for the first time—patterns of everyday interaction that any normal, healthy family enjoys.

Each home has six children, ranging up to eighteen years of age, usually with a mix of boys and girls. The homes are established in residential neighborhoods and are indistinguishable from surrounding homes. The children attend local schools, become involved in local activities, make friends with neighborhood kids, and become part of just another family on the block. For many of these children, it is the first time they have ever had a home as nice as the other kids, the first time they have ever felt a part of the community, the first time they have ever felt they really belonged.

Central to the model are the carefully chosen, professionally trained family-care parents who are supported by a staff that includes a director, a school coordinator, a social worker, a psychiatrist, a psychologist, and others as needed.

Since that night twenty-five years ago, I have never stopped thinking about or working on concepts related to parenting. I have participated in the development of three separate demonstration projects, two of which are national in scope. Because of my work I have dealt firsthand with the worst and the best of parenting. These projects were not clinical laboratories, but real homes with real youngsters learning how to be loved and structured. The remarkable couples working with us helped identify the key ingredients in proper parenting. Bad parenting causes damage, but the cure is not found in hospitals or prisons, it is found in environments where good parenting can take place. The cure is found in good homes where mothers and fathers become caring authority figures.

The human animal cannot become a whole, healthy adult if it is denied exposure to mature parental figures. It is the simplest of concepts, but one that many people have forgotten, or ignore.

The surrogate homes we have established are good and the family-care parents who make our concept work are extraordinarily compassionate, but in the process of creating this surrogate design, I have learned that *the best environment in which to raise a child is the home of the biological parent.* There is no substitute that can compare in quality of care, if mothers and fathers are willing to make the effort to acquire the skills to parent.

The complexities of our society require a new level of commitment from those of us who decide to make babies. If you want successful children who will grow to become content, secure adults, there are new skills to be learned. Passive, shoot-from-the-hip parenting is a luxury of days gone by.

A doctor friend told me of the tremendous advances made in surgical techniques and equipment during periods of war. The sheer numbers of casualties and the need for prompt, efficient care brought about knowledge that would never have been discovered in any other circumstance. I, too, have witnessed and directed skilled professionals in a battle zone. We take six confused, hurt, angry kids out of mental hospitals, reform schools, and broken homes and hire a couple that is willing to love, provide care, and create a family. I have learned concepts in parenting that would not have been possible anywhere else. What we live through with these children is both traumatic and exciting, but what we learn in the process is the essence of parenting.

To write a "how to" book is the ultimate presumption, especially when one presumes to tell others how to care for their children. I do so, however, with a true sense of humility and my honest belief that the knowledge will benefit others.

This book is my heartfelt response to the requests made by parents who have experienced the loss of a child, and who have asked me to tell others what they have learned as a result of their tragedy. These are not pontifical thoughts passed down from the ivory tower of intellectual isolation. Much of what I have learned is the direct result of mistakes I have made while raising my own five children. I can thank some higher power that so far my offspring have survived and prospered, in spite of my mistakes.

The opportunity to provide care and nurturance to a child can be a beautiful experience, but if we persist in ignoring some basic rules, we could destroy that which we love most.

When I give speeches around the country, young parents invariably come up to me afterward and ask if the kids who fail in our society are not the product of bad people who happen to be parents. When I tell them that good people can be bad parents, they look shocked and frightened.

If you want emotionally healthy kids, you need to become active, knowledgeable parents. I fervently hope that this book will help that process.

1

Good parenting is not a natural but a learned process.

When you consider buying a new car, one of the first things you investigate is the basic equipment—those items that come with each car in that particular model. One of the common misconceptions is that good parenting skills are a part of our basic equipment. We believe that each and every one of us is born with these skills. Wrong.

Being a good parent requires as much time, talent, energy, and thought as any full-time job. I would like to include training in this list of requirements, but unfortunately, few educational resources exist. We therefore are responsible for our own parental training and skill development.

What do I mean when I say "Parenting requires thought"? Let me go from the simple to the complex. My fifth child, Nicholas Alexander, was sixteen months old when he walked into the bathroom and began to play with the hair dryer. I did not react, because the dryer was not plugged in and, therefore, not dangerous. The next day he returned and again pulled the dryer off the counter, but this time I yelled at him. The dryer was plugged in. Nicholas was confused, and I was at fault. A sixteen-month-old child does not know the difference between a safe appliance and a potentially lethal one. I was giving mixed messages and was not thinking when I allowed him to play with it the first day. My son will not grow up to become the next Al Capone because I gave a mixed message, at least I hope not, but given enough misinformation any child will become confused, frustrated, and eventually angry. If I, as a parent, continue to lackadaisically confuse Nicholas with bad input, he will be neurotic. I had let my guard down. I was not thinking.

I was on a flight to Miami recently and found myself sitting next to a distinguished-looking gentleman. He was one of those men whose carriage denotes power and prestige, and I remember wondering how people like him never wrinkle their suits or spill soup on their ties. Not long after we took off we began to talk, and he asked what line of work I was in. When I told him, he flinched and turned away to stare out the window. In the split second it took to turn away, his expression had gone from pleasant to pained. Several minutes went by, and I was rummaging through my briefcase looking for a book when he turned back. He apologized for his apparent rudeness and, without a pause, told me about the loss of his seventeen-year-old son.

The man talking to me was now vulnerable and hurt. The conversation had shifted from a lighthearted chat to an intense confession. His description of Robert Jr. made him sound like a fairly average seventeen-year-old. According to his father, Robert Jr. was respectful and diligent in his responsibilities up to his fifteenth birthday, but soon thereafter he started to talk back and break some of the rules. Two days after young Robert's seventeenth birthday, Robert Sr. found a seemingly logical pamphlet describing an organization for parents called Tough Love. The notion espoused in the one-page pamphlet was simple and logical: Tell your kid what the rules are and that he has a choice of following the rules or going out on his own. He went straight home, confronted his son, and has not seen him since. By this time the man had tears in his eyes, and he apologized for burdening me with his problems.

I asked him what line of work he was in. He resisted the shift in conversation, fearing I was avoiding his problem. I assured him that we would get back to his son, but begged his indulgence with my diversion. Robert Sr. was a senior executive in one of America's largest corporations. I asked him to describe some of the problems he has with other executives within the company. One particular problem was complex and obviously difficult to solve. I asked him to tell me what he did to resolve the problem.

"The same thing we usually do," he replied. "We called in some consultants, did the necessary research, held several high-level executive sessions, and, and . . ." He looked at me and laughed. "You people have a sinister way of making your point."

My point was very simple, and you do not have to be a corporate executive to understand the issue. In our society we do not consider parenting a manageable process or a learned skill. I told Robert Sr. that being a parent requires as much active management, thought, and consideration as his job. He leaned away from me and squinted down his nose as if seeing me for the first time. The notion I had just proposed was novel if not preposterous to him. He acknowledged that his family was more important than his work, but felt that it would be impossible to devote an equal portion of energy.

"When you thought you were having problems with your son, how many consultants did you call in? How much research did you do? What was going on at school? What was happening with your son's girlfriend? What was your son doing with his spare time? How many family meetings did you call?" He shook his head and looked at his hands.

When we have problems at work, we call everyone together, sit down around a table, and discuss the issue. You would be amazed at the number of problems that can be solved by confronting the issues. But we do not do it with our families. We think family problems will solve themselves. They don't, they simply fester. Robert Sr. was now curious and wanted to know what a consultant could have done. I explained that a good professional would have provided, through observation, some insights that might have allowed him and his son to resolve their differences. He asked for an example, and it was my turn to laugh. If I were completely ethical, I would have respectfully declined, professing a lack of information, but I had a hunch I was eager to put to the test.

"What were you like when you were seventeen years old?" I asked. He huffed and puffed for several seconds before he said, "That's different. My dad was a rigid old dinosaur. He mellowed out later on, but I left home as soon as I was eighteen." We had landed and we were about to get off the plane when he asked if I thought his son thought he was a "rigid old dinosaur."

The purpose of my trip to Miami was to give a speech. As a direct result of the conversation with Robert Sr., I emphasized in my speech the need to be thinking parents. After the talk, one very honest woman stood up and said that when she came home from work she was exhausted and resented the demands placed on her by her children and spouse. I told her she needed to pace herself at work or change jobs. The most important half of her life was being shortchanged.

By the time I got home I wished desperately that I had the young woman's address. I would have liked to have written and apologized for my glib response to her honest dilemma. It is difficult to parent when the stress level of survival has risen drastically in the last twenty years. If you want to live in the same type of community you grew up in so that your children will have the same advantages you had, it now requires two paychecks instead of one.

Our parents taught most of us that the tasks of cooking, cleaning, and child care are the responsibilities of women. Even though most mothers now have full-time careers outside the home, their parenting job description has not changed. We may pay lip service to the notion of shared household and parenting responsibilities, but family behavior patterns traditionally lag behind societal changes in behavior. In this case, children are being shortchanged because it is difficult for women to assume both roles, and the children begin to feel like burdens that neither parent has time for. If a mother is tired and stressed, the entire family is affected.

Mothering and fathering are not the same jobs today's parents remember. If two adults decide they want to work and have children, who does what? The children still need to be parented. The family will continue to need to function as a cohesive unit, and it will require some thought and leadership.

I am convinced that once we adjust to our new lifestyles, we can do the jobs associated with mothering and fathering better than our parents did. But we must redefine how we will do the same job under different circumstances. Many of us are muddling along wondering why our house doesn't feel like a home.

One of the advantages inherent in these new expectations is the expansion of the father's role. These days, a man can get intimately involved with child rearing and not be considered a wimp. Most of the work we do to support ourselves is dull compared with the adventures of being with our children and watching them learn. For generations we have lingered on the perimeter of this privilege.

Before I get too enthusiastic with my predictions for a brighter future, however, we need to *think through* just how we are going to parent under these new circumstances. I was forced to confront these concerns several years ago when I was manipulated into a neighborhood family's crisis.

Pam and Bill were friends of a friend. They had three daughters, and their oldest, April, was thirteen when our mutual friend Helen came to our house to ask for my help on their behalf. I was afraid Helen was going to hyperventilate when I opened the door. The problem came out in a breathless rush of words before I could even invite her in. According to Helen, Pam, Bill, and the three girls were the perfect family. Having never seen a perfect family, I was enticed into listening to the whole story. After some interruptions to ask questions, I was able to unscramble the story enough to learn that this perfect family had a pregnant thirteen-year-old daughter, and was now tainted by the shame. Helen was very dramatic, and I am not making fun of this family, but as I think back on that Sunday morning and her descriptions, I can't help but laugh.

The parents were devastated, the daughter had decided to run away and had informed her parents of her intent. The only person they could turn to for advice was Helen, which in itself was a frightening circumstance. I gave her the name of a good family therapist, and advised that they make contact first thing Monday morning. Helen was back in an hour to tell me they had made several decisions, none of which included going to a family therapist. The most frightening decision involved shipping April off to a great aunt in Canada to have the baby. Apparently the great aunt in Toronto was farther away than any other relative they could think of. April and the great aunt had never met. Bill and Pam wished to meet with me that afternoon at a local pancake house. According to Helen, they wanted to hear my opinion of the decisions they had made. The whole episode was getting crazier, but it was becoming obvious that the drama was a Helen production. I didn't go to meet them at the pancake house, but did say I would meet them at my home at one o'clock, on the condition that Helen would introduce them and then leave. It was no longer funny.

My first shock was the discovery that these were not stupid people. Pam was a history teacher at the local high school, Bill was the coordinator at the city planning department, and their daughter April was mature, attractive, and the most rational of the three. They were professional, intelligent people, but like many parents in a crisis situation, they had switched off their thinking capacity.

To begin with, confiding in and consulting with Helen was not appropriate. She was a notorious neighborhood gossip. We all loved her, but her propensity to tell everyone's secrets was so pronounced that we would tease her about it and she would giggle. Coffee with Helen was your opportunity to pass on any message that you wanted to get to the neighbors. She had the emotional maturity of a twelve-year-old. In the midst of a very real family trauma, Helen was not a logical consultant. As it turned out, the Canada plan was Helen's idea. She had a cousin who was sent to Idaho to have her baby, and it had worked out fine. Like the gentleman I had met on the plane, who had given his son an ultimatum after picking up a pamphlet on the street, these people, without thinking, were making precipitous decisions that would have a major impact on their daughter.

After an uncomfortable introduction and a retelling of the initial problem, I asked the parents why they had rejected my suggestion to see a professional family therapist before they made any decisions. Their response was typical. "If we see a therapist, everyone will think we are crazy." I pointed out that they were about to send their child off to a stranger, to live through an extremely traumatic event, and the negative effect could be profound and permanent. While I was talking Bill kept looking at me and then, without turning his head, rolling his eyes in April's direction. He was telling me with his expressions not to say such things in front of his daughter.

I asked Bill to say what was on his mind. He started to blush, and April said, "My father doesn't want to you say things like that in front of me. I am a nonperson, and therefore incapable of being involved in what is happening to me, my baby, or my body." Her statement broke the ice, and we began to talk. I had originally anticipated giving a forty-minute lecture on the importance of thinking this thing through with the help of professionals, but as it turned out, we spent the afternoon together, and they stayed for dinner.

Pam, Bill, and the three girls had become what I call a paper doll family. They all had a very definite image of what a family should look like. Helen had introduced them as the "perfect" family. But it was a facade for the benefit of the outside world. Their family motto should have been: "If you have a problem, bury it. Don't let the neighbors know, and for God's sake don't share it with your parents."

As parents, we tell our children how we want them to behave by what we say and don't say. In the paper doll families, the parents tell their children to bury their problems and concerns. Don't expose your dirty laundry to me or the world, and everything will be all right. The children do their best to meet these expectations, but the unsolved, untouched problems will someday reach a critical mass, and no one will be prepared for the consequences. The pregnancy was the least of this family's problems.

Bill and Pam had a two-career marriage with no energy left over for parenting. April described her mother coming home from school tired and angry. Her father would come in, pick up the paper, and wait for April to call him to dinner. No one talked, and when the kids tried to tell of their concerns the parents said they were too tired. After listening to the whole scenario, it was obvious that thirteen-year-old April had taken on the traditional mother's role. She took care of the other girls, cooked dinner, made love, and had babies. On a day-to-day basis, she spent more time thinking about issues of parenting than did her mother or father.

When the crisis happened, Pam and Bill were totally unprepared to deal with it. Their parenting skills were rusty, and they turned to the neighborhood busybody for consultation. During our talk April told of the problems her two younger sisters were having, and Pam broke down, saying it was all her fault. Bill tried to make her feel better by saying he was as guilty as she was. I fixed coffee and April came in to meet the rest of my family. After they had their cry, we began to talk about some of the things they needed to be thinking about. Seeking help from a real professional was an absolute essential. They agreed, and did so the next day.

They called five months later and asked if they could come over. They gave me a beautiful bottle of wine, and Pam gave me a big hug. They had been and were still in family therapy. Apparently, the therapist had opened a Pandora's box, and when all of the family issues were exposed, both parents were amazed that their kids had survived their incompetent nonparticipation in family affairs. April and her parents were considering an abortion when she miscarried.

This fragile group of individuals did become a successful family with all the kinks and faults that all successful families have. But it didn't come without work, and it is true that healthy families are not especially pretty. They argue when they have a point to make. They shout when they need to be heard. They cry big sloppy tears all over each other when they hurt.

The therapist suggested that Bill use some of his organizational skills to develop a family work chart. They divided up the shopping, cooking, cleaning, tutoring, and chauffeuring. Everyone did his fair share.

They set a time aside to have family talks, and were not only allowed but were encouraged to say what was hurting or feeling good in their lives. They practiced these sessions in therapy before they tried them at home on their own.

The two younger girls were having school problems, and when Pam asked the therapist how they should handle it, he laughed and told her to come up with the solution since she was the professional educator. She ended up following the same advice she gave other parents when they came to her asking for help with their failing children. I never did find out what Pam's solution was, but I do know that one of the most common failures in parenting is the reluctance of parents to actively interact with the school.

I don't know what your family's problems are, but I do know you can't hide them, and most of them will not go away when they are ignored. It should not be difficult to find a good family therapist through your family doctor or local mental health society. And if some of your friends think you are crazy, tell them to climb out of the dark ages. Your family's mental health is far more important than maintaining the respect of ignorant friends.

If you parent properly you will need to use your imagination and intelligence. Don't be afraid to confront issues and ask hard questions of each other. If things feel bad, and the walls are closing in on you, do something. Some people seem to have a sacrosanct reverence for the family, and when it begins to crack they treat it gingerly, as though it were rare china. Others are so preoccupied they wouldn't know a family problem if it stomped all over them. These people have the notion that their family comes first, but behave as though they couldn't care less.

I have a friend who is a bartender in a fancy bar next to a large hotel in Chicago. I was kidding him about being the drunk's psychiatrist. He didn't laugh, and said that most of the crying came from sixty-year-old men who had lost their families. He said, "If you want to see something pathetic, come and listen to these supposedly successful men tell how they didn't know their family was important until it was gone, and now they are getting old and no one cares."

How often do we use the phrase "the demands of family." The word "demands" connotes an unwanted chore, a heavy burden. If you feel that the care and feeding of the group of people living under your roof has become a burden, you are probably right. You might want to rethink your job descriptions to reallocate the load.

When you have a family conference to assign these

tasks, think of your house as a community of independent human beings who have agreed to live together and share the responsibilities. When we use the term "family" to describe the group, all kinds of traditions, guilt feelings, and assumptions inhibit free thinking.

Who does what? Sit down and list the actual jobs from laundry to cooking. Decide which ones you like least and which you like most. If there are tasks that you prefer that no one else likes, you get them. For those jobs no one wants, divide them equally among the participants, and rotate these responsibilities on a monthly basis. The chores you get always seem hardest, but with the rotation, there is rest from the misery.

A monthly meeting should be scheduled to reassign jobs and discuss adjustments. In the beginning, the group will fall into traditional behaviors. The mothering person will continue to pick up after the others, and the slacker will forget on a regular basis. For the first few months this change, like all change, will be uncomfortable, but if you stick with it, everyone will begin to see its value. If the lazy one continues to ignore her responsibility, hire it out, and make the recalcitrant family member pay for the work done. This contingency should be understood from the beginning.

Don't assume that all household chores need to be done by family members in order to have a real family. There is nothing sacrilegious about hiring out the house cleaning, laundry, or yard work if you can afford it.

If you are moving, choose an environment that is truly compatible with your family. If you don't like maintaining a house and yard, explore the possibility of living in a condominium. We moved two years ago. I hate yard work and love golf. The two don't go together. I found a house affiliated with a neighborhood association that mows the lawn in the summer and removes the snow in the winter.

I started this chapter talking about parenting skills, and stating that being a good parent requires as much time, talent, and energy as a full-time job. You have to be as skilled at organizing your household as you do your area of responsibility in the workplace. You need to be as flexible and imaginative when solving family problems as you are when solving problems on the job.

We live in an exciting world that is rapidly changing. Our concept of parenting will keep pace with these changes if we approach raising a child as a stimulating new challenge.

2

Good parents know how to instill the value of delayed gratification.

Have you ever heard parents or grandparents say, "I know I give them too much and spoil them rotten, but you're only young once"?

Unfortunately, they are right. We are only young once, but it is while we are young that we learn most: Our patterns of behavior are established, and our understanding of the world around us is crystallized. When we give to our children indiscriminately, they believe that things, comfort, and entertainment are theirs for the asking. They believe that the child's role is to take and the parents' job is to give. We teach them to be selfish and self-centered, then wonder why our adolescents are selfish and self-centered.

When they are young their wants are simple and affordable, but as they mature their requests become less cute and more abrasive. The plea for an ice cream cone is replaced by the demand for a car. The tearful appeal for a doll becomes a screaming, hysterical, insistent petition for a ski trip. We, the parents, look at each other and shake our heads in perplexed wonder: "Where did this monster of consumption come from?" The child and the problem come from us.

By this time our children are convinced that the world is their playground and that if there is a bill, someone else will pick it up. The bad habits they have learned have far-reaching consequences. When the parents are financially and emotionally drained, and as a result are forced to say "no," many of these children steal what they want and are then confused when the police say they have to give it back and pay the consequences.

To say they are confused, angry, and hurt when they are punished for stealing may sound ridiculous, but keep in mind that the overindulged child has been taught to believe that his wishes and needs come first. When the parents say "no," he is hurt because someone changed the rules. All those possessions represented love to the child, and when they are denied, he experiences a tremendous loss. These are the students who quit school because "It's not fun anymore." They do not comprehend the concept of delayed gratification. They do not realize that someday the education they gave up will be needed to enable them to support themselves.

Why do we spoil our kids? If we took a survey on a street of any American city, and asked a hundred people if they thought it wise to overindulge children, at least ninety-five of them would say no. Yet most of us are guilty of this to some degree.

We do it to buy love: "If I don't give her the doll, she will think I don't love her."

We do it to buy peace: "I would rather buy the ice cream cone than have him throw a fit and embarrass me in front of those other people."

We do it because we are proud: "If Mary next door can have a deluxe dollhouse, by God my Suzie can have one, too, even if we can't afford it. My kids are going to have it better than I had it when I was growing up."

We do it because we are lazy. We tell our spouses, "Go ahead and get it. I don't have the time to explain why he shouldn't have it."

We do it to assuage our guilt.

We buy things as a substitute for our time. We would rather be working or playing golf, and we try to convince ourselves and our children that dollars and things are just as important as our time and energy. We rob our children of a needed relationship and send them off into a competitive, complicated world believing that love is wrapped in packages or carried in a billfold.

When I talk to young people in prisons, reform schools, or mental hospitals, they often refer to the emptiness they feel inside. If asked what could fill that empty space, they shake their heads and say they don't know. If the child is not exposed to honest parental involvement, he or she has no point of reference, no understanding, only a sense of loss, and so the child grasps again for dollars.

It did not begin as a case. A friend, John W., called to ask when I would be going to the West Coast; he needed a favor. I said I was leaving in two days and that my schedule was packed, but I made the mistake of asking what he wanted. My friend stated that a colleague of his on the West Coast had called in a panic. His daughter was being imprisoned in a hospital for the criminally insane, but she was not insane. When I asked for details, John said he didn't know. He then asked if I would make arrangements to see them and find out what was going on.

I took the colleague's name and phone number but made no promises. Curiosity is a powerful force, and in my case it's an awesome motivator: People and the fixes in which they trap themselves are a never-ending source of mystery and interest. When I arrived on the coast, I extended the trip thirty-six hours and made the call, as my friend, John W., knew I would.

Paul Hollingsworth was a father in extreme distress. His description of the problem was so garbled I was still not aware of the details of the case when Becky walked through the door of the visiting room, sneered at her parents, and asked who I was. Her parents, Paul and Sarah Hollingsworth, were attractive people, so I was not surprised when Becky turned out to be a beautiful girl, but I was shocked by other aspects of her appearance. This sixteen-year-old child looked like an angry twenty-year-old prostitute without makeup. Her body language indicated indifferent hostility, and she turned her back on her parents when she spoke: "I really don't care who you are if you can get me out of here. These people," Becky jerked her thumb toward her parents without looking at them, "are not doing me any good. Maybe you have enough brains to get something done."

Before the child had come into the room I had asked the parents to tell me what was going on. But Sarah broke down in tears and Paul was attempting to comfort her when Becky was escorted in. I still did not know the specifics, but even without their story, I was fairly certain I could have written an accurate case summary. It did not take a genius to realize I was dealing with an overindulged child and some very confused parents. I sent Becky back to the ward, told Sarah to get some fresh air, and asked Paul to tell me what had happened.

Two months earlier, Becky and an eighteen-year-old boyfriend got drunk and destroyed her new car. It was the second car and the second drunk driving violation in four months. Becky was at the wheel when she took a curve too fast and ran head-on into a car carrying a young family. She killed the mother and a six-month-old baby. This time, the best attorneys in town and all the assurances from her respected parents could not excuse Becky's mistake.

Her attorney knew they were in trouble. He convinced Sarah and Paul that Becky should plead insanity, and he would attempt to persuade the judge to allow her to be admitted to the finest psychiatric institution available. The judge was only half convinced. He accepted the insanity plea, but he then committed Becky to the maximum security unit of the state hospital for the criminally insane. Her attorney had wanted the insanity plea to avoid a commitment to the girls' reform school or the women's prison, both of which looked like country clubs compared to that particular unit of the state hospital. The attorney's plan had backfired.

Sarah came back from her walk. She was composed and was able to describe Becky's childhood to me. Three months after Becky was born, Sarah had hired a nanny and then had gone back to work. She was a skilled corporate lawyer with an established practice. Paul traveled most of the week as a management consultant but came home on weekends. The first nanny lasted four years, the second one year, and the third five months. From then on it was a series of baby-sitters and live-in servants. According to her parents, Becky was fine until she was nine. Paul said it was a simple matter of having a mind of her own. Sarah said she was just a little headstrong, but nothing bad.

When I asked what had happened when she was nine, they looked at each other before telling me that she had killed a friend's kitty. She wanted the kitty and the friend refused so she killed it. When she was thirteen Becky asked her parents if she could go with her sixteen-year-old friends to San Francisco for a weekend rock concert. They told her no. As far as either parent could remember it was the first time they had adamantly refused a request. Becky ran away and was gone for two weeks. She was found in San Francisco living in an apartment with two twenty-three-year-old men. The credit card bills came in a few weeks later—they added up to just over $4,000.

Later that evening I talked with Becky. She was not homesick, showed absolutely no remorse for the role she had played in the death of the mother and child, and was convinced that the rain-slick streets were the real culprits, not her.

Rebecca Lodge Hollingsworth was a mess, a totally screwed-up, snotty brat. She was the purest example of overindulgence I had ever come across. Intellectually, I could empathize with her circumstances. Professionally, I could see why Becky behaved the way she did. Personally, I found her very difficult to like.

By the end of the second day I had talked with Becky three times and met with her treatment team twice. In the wrap-up session, Sarah and Paul walked into the waiting room I was using as an office. They looked hurt and angry. John W. had labeled me a child advocate, and from that the Hollingsworths had assumed I would automatically do whatever the "child" wanted.

It had become obvious, however, by the questions I had asked and the respect I had shown the hospital staff that I was not a white knight who had ridden in to condemn the horrid facility and save the young damsel in distress. Judging from the expressions on their faces, I was not at all sure they were going to sit still long enough to listen to my recommendations, but when I told them I had made contact with one of the best clinicians in the area and she had agreed to work on the case, they brightened. Sarah jumped right in and asked if I could convince the judge to release Becky to this person's care.

They were missing the point. As I explained the hard facts, the blood drained from Sarah's face and Paul turned away and stared at the wall. As much as I wanted to soften the blow, it was not possible. Becky was where she belonged. The treatment team was truly professional and as compassionate as any group of humans could be to a child who had rejected and detested any of their attempts to work with her. The secure hospital environment was safe, and Becky was protected from the other inmates; just as important, the other inmates were protected from Becky.

The clinician I hired was a family therapist who had agreed to work with Sarah and Paul. In spite of the seriousness of the offense, Becky would someday be released, and the Hollingsworths were in dire need of a parenting education.

Sarah asked if I thought they were bad parents. I said no, they were not bad parents, they simply had never assumed the role of parents. Sarah and Paul had not only abdicated their responsibility they had never given the job to anyone else. It is one thing to say that you do not want to parent, but it is quite another to avoid designating a substitute.

What they did could be equated to taking a baby lioness into a protected valley and giving it all the food it wanted to eat, but, when it was grown, turning it loose in the wild and expecting it to survive. By giving her everything she wanted, when she wanted it, they had deskilled their daughter. More important, they had given indiscriminately, taking away the joy that can only come when one works for a goal. At the age of sixteen, Becky was bored. She had tried cars, sex, and drugs and was searching madly for a new thrill when the court interrupted her desperation.

Paul and Sarah Hollingsworth had created a human being for whom only the most compassionate could feel sorry. The criminal who was beaten and starved as a child can and does elicit understanding, but according to our societal mores, Becky had every advantage. Few people, including the judge, would acknowledge the reality of Becky's neglect.

The Hollingsworths were not bad people, and the neglect did not occur because both parents worked. Paul and Sarah gave too much, expected too little, and ignored the basic structures that would have given their daughter a sense of responsibility.

When I started to write this chapter and thought back through the classic cases that would illustrate overindulgence, Becky and her parents came immediately to mind. The Hollingsworth family is a cliché, and the fact that they were the most prominent in my memory betrays my own prejudice. We all know that people who have lots of money tend to spoil their kids. When these kids turn out bad, those of us who are financially less fortunate seem to relish a certain vindictive joy as we perceive this to be one of the few woes of the rich. The notion that only the wealthy overindulge their children, however, is an illusion.

Wealth has little or nothing to do with the problem. I had worked with delinquents for several years before it dawned on me that many who came from abject poverty were overindulged children. "I Want What I Want When I Want It" could have been the theme song for many of these wayward waifs who came to us incapable of understanding delayed gratification. In the case of unsupervised adolescents who eventually become delinquents, they learn to gratify their own needs. They eat when they are hungry and can find food. They steal toys to entertain themselves. They watch television whenever they want. The unfortunate fact remains that the pampered child and the unsupervised delinquent who steals to survive often end up with the same personality traits because, by whatever means, they have both been overindulged and given no real structure.

Several months ago I was conducting an evaluation and consultation with the staff of our Arizona project. Part of the project involves a group of volatile, exciting, unpredictable women who work as parent aides. They do remarkable work with children and their biological families in the families' own homes. In most cases courts use the parent aides as the last resort before removing the child from the home. I have learned much from these specialized professionals who walk into disrupted homes, develop caring relationships, and teach a dysfunctional group of individuals to operate as a family. During this particular consultation, we were talking about issues of poverty when one of the aides told of a recent experience that illustrates the notion that even the poor who do care for and supervise their children can overindulge them.

Nancy, the parent aide, was going on her first visit to a new case. She described the house as a small frame structure that had not been painted in years. The porch leaned to one side, and the yard was littered with trash. The first thing that caught her eye as she picked her way up the broken steps was a notice from the gas service company stapled to the one support post that was still standing. It informed the occupant that if the gas bill was not paid by a designated date, the gas would be turned off. It was January, and cold, and the turnoff deadline was three days away. The family consisted of a middle-aged mother and her twelve-year-old son. Mrs. P. and her son, David, lived on a welfare payment of $300 per month. The check had arrived the day before, and Mrs. P. and David had just returned from the store, where she had spent $142 on the best soccer equipment available.

Nancy tried to talk to Mrs. P. about the inadvisability of spending that kind of money on soccer equipment when she had not yet paid the rent, the gas bill, or left enough for food. But she couldn't keep the mother's attention. David kept interrupting them as they talked demanding that he and his mother leave immediately to buy the sweatbands she had forgotten. Nancy finally sent the boy outside and confronted his mother with her irrational behavior. Mrs. P. began to cry and admitted she was irresponsible, but explained that David was all she had left. Her husband was dead, and she had no other relatives. Even though they were poor, her son was going to "have it as good as them other kids."

Mrs. P's motives were no different than yours or mine. We want our kids to have the best. We live in a society where having the best designates our value. We have allowed the promoters of purchasable goods to dictate and set our standards of self-worth. Mrs. P. was also pressured by the notion that she could lose the love of her son if she did not give in to his demands.

All of us are capable of overindulgence, but we are also capable of change. We can change our habits as well as our values. The primary issue is not *how much* you give, but *how* you give. The "how" is, in reality, the culprit.

Few things in life are more disturbing than to go to a grocery store and witness a child throwing a fit about something he wants. It is embarrassing to the parent and disruptive to everyone else within a three-block radius. This pattern of behavior is stimulated by our response to the child's request. When the child asks, we give. Junior asks for a cookie, we pull the box off the shelf, tear it open, give him the cookie, and continue with our shopping. The moment we opened the package or gave the child the product to hold, we set a precedent as valid as any given in a law book. We are saying, by our response to the child's request, that this is the way to get what you want, and this is how we will give it to you. The next time he asks for the cookie and we say "no," the child is justifiably confused and angry. *We* broke the rule.

Our two-year-old son Nicholas is a Life Saver addict, and we buy them for him. Not only are they tasty, but we can teach him his colors when he asks for one. But the purchase and distribution of the candy is carried out according to consistent guidelines. We pick up the Life Savers, put them in the basket, and he does not touch them until we get home. This is the first lesson in delayed gratification. If we buy a toy in his presence, the toy is paid for and taken home before he plays with it. Nicholas does not feel any real urgency when he sees something he wants, because the object will not be given to him immediately and he knows it.

Before my older children hurt themselves laughing while they read this, let me confess that I have always been softhearted, and it is not easy for me to deny them any request. Not long ago my wife, Nicholas, and I went to the store and were trying to decide if the grapes were sweet. I picked one up and tasted it. Nicholas watched this illegal transaction with interest and then asked for one himself. I gave him a grape and forgot the incident until our next visit to the grocery store. We were next to the fruit stand when he began to yell for a grape. I paid for my transgression, but it was a good reminder that our children do learn what we teach.

When your child throws one of these hysterical fits in the store (and note I say when, not if), there is one cure that seems to work. Leave the shopping cart where it is, walk outside, keep calm, talk quietly, and stay outside until the child settles down. You can swat their pants until you are blue in the face, but as a rule it only stimulates the volume, compounds your embarrassment, and hurts your hand as well as your child.

Shopping for food, clothes, and toys is a national pastime. We may be, as some poverty-stricken third-world countries claim, a society of spoiled people, but the fact remains that we have our toys and we enjoy buying them. I was in Phoenix recently when an old man in a beautiful red sports car whizzed by. Attached to the car was a bumper sticker that read "He Who Dies With the Most Toys Wins!" I laughed and wanted to cheer him on. I am not preaching the virtues of "commodity abstinence"; I am saying that some people are programmed at an early age to purchase impulsively, and that can be destructive. When material objects become our sole confirmation of self-worth, we are in trouble.

I would guess the old man worked very hard for his red sports car and deserved the buzz he was getting. The impulse buyer, on the other hand, does not think of budgets, or real need; he buys to satisfy an emotional hunger, even though the satisfaction that he receives is only temporary. The existence of the impulse buyer has given rise to a whole new concept in marketing. The next time you are in a store, look at the host of products within easy reach at the checkout stand: candy, gum, cute little flashlights, the latest gadget. To those of us who learned at an early age to be impulse buyers, such things can come to represent love and security.

Credit cards are the perfect example of our need to get what we want when we want it. Our wants are often determined by our need to confirm our self-worth. But we are not the first nor will we be the last generation to determine self-worth by the clothes we wear, or the house we live in, or the perfumed scent that announces our exclusivity. The radical youth of the sixties tried to break from these long-held standards, but our desire for material comforts won out, and so exclusive name brands came back with a vengeance.

I am not judging this human characteristic, but I am saying that the motivations that drive the overindulged child do not spring from a vacuum. The human animal has this primeval need to establish class and position. Children are influenced by societal mores established long before they sucked in that first breath of life-giving air. It is their *method* of acquiring these status symbols that has become a problem. When I grew up I wanted the good life, and the good things that went with it, but there was never a question in my mind about where it was going to come from. It is the parents' responsibility to teach their children to delay gratification, to work for goals, and to resist the impulse to have their wants satisfied immediately. The real question is: How do you accomplish this seemingly impossible feat after the fact?

Over the years I have watched many of the family-care parents in our projects teach children, most of whom were in their late adolescence, to change a lifetime of compulsive behavior. It can be done, and in one case I watched with interest as one of our toughest kids was transformed into a gentleman and a scholar.

J. J. Heart was a big woman, and her husband, John, even though he looked average in most settings, was dwarfed by his large spouse. John and J.J. were family-care parents in one of our first demonstration projects developed in the Midwest over twenty years ago. At the time we had ten children in each of the new homes that we had constructed specifically for the project. Today we have a limit of six children in each home, and so we cannot imagine how we got by with ten, but we did and the Hearts thrived in this chaotic household.

Lewis P. was fifteen when he was referred to us by the juvenile court. He was big, strong, and angry. Lewis was a perfect example of the self-indulged delinquent: He got what he wanted because he took it. The only reason I considered accepting this aggressive young man was that an opening existed in the Heart House. If anyone could handle him, John and J.J. could. J.J. was the primary parent and disciplinarian. She was a happy person and had a funny habit of singing her answers or commands in a vibrating falsetto that could be heard in three counties. Lewis let it be known when he walked in the door that he was not going to follow any of the "fucking rules" and that if she stayed out of his way he would stay out of hers. I took his arm and started to lead him back to the car. J.J. stopped me, however, and said that she was willing to give him a try. Lewis didn't seem to care one way or the other. He simply shrugged and walked back to the house.

I watched him and the household closely over the next several days. Like all good family couples, the Hearts maintained a fairly tight structure. Beds were made and rooms were cleaned before the children came down for breakfast. Homework was done before play or television. Meals were served on time and attended by everyone on time. The shared cleanup and maintenance chores were completed daily. There was a routine in the house, a rhythm that enabled this large group of people to live together.

During most of the first week, J.J. did not ask Lewis to do anything. She literally left him alone. He followed none of the rules, and she didn't ask him to. He would sit slouched in front of the television while the other children ignored his brooding presence. After a while, this obvious disparity was too much, and he asked why she didn't ask him to do what the others kids had to do. She told him that she wanted him to observe the other children, and now that he had asked, it was time to begin to participate in the daily activities of the household and to become part of its structure.

Lewis had observed several things that first week while he was trying to hide behind his nonchalance. The other kids liked J.J. and John. When she told them to do something, she was not angry. Everyone in the house seemed happy. When he tried to create a split between the children and the Hearts, the kids laughed and told him to get lost.

J.J.'s procedures and expectations were simple, and not artificial. Twelve people lived in one house, and if those individuals were going to function as a unit without getting in each other's way, each would have to carry part of the load. If you wanted to watch TV, you had to do your chores. If you wanted to play, you had to finish your homework. I could be outside and still hear her off-key soprano: "No, not until you clean up the dishes."

Lewis, like most of the children in her home, resisted and tested her, but each month the reports got better. It took the better part of a year to reach a point where Lewis could be considered a part of the household. It took one long year to reach a point where Lewis could function without blowing up when his needs were not immediately met. I hear parents describe the habits of their own spoiled children, and when I suggest setting some limits, they say, "I did that two weeks ago and it didn't work."

A pattern of behavior established over a lifetime will not change with a few commands. But if you are serious about moderating your child's behavior, you can start by sitting him down and talking about the fact that things are going to change. Do not do it after a confrontation. One of J.J.'s secrets of success was her happy countenance. All too often we get angry before we even ask our children to do something. We anticipate resistance, and so we get mad before the child has a chance to respond. In this suggested family conference, you need to let the child know that new rules will be in effect. It will require some changes, and everyone will be going through some adjustments.

The onslaught of adolescence is usually the point at which most parents feel that something is terribly wrong. The abrasive demands often become intolerable, the confrontations frightening. I remember the first time I recommended that a family sit down and confront their teenage son. During this experience I realized this adolescent was dealing with a reality that we adults were ignoring. I even understood how his negative response to us was logical. Let me illustrate this.

Carl and Liz were old friends, and when they found out that my family and I were moving to their community they invited me to stay in their home while I looked for a house. They had two children, Tom, who was fifteen, and Jack, who was twelve. Tom and Jack were bright, attractive, and, for the most part, well-behaved kids. We were having dinner on the third night of my stay when Tom asked for a motorbike. His request was so casual that I wasn't sure he hadn't asked for the potatoes. Liz excused herself, saying she had to get dessert, and Carl asked Tom why he thought he needed a motorbike.

As it turned out, every single kid in the neighborhood had a motorbike, and Tom had held off as long as he could, but the time had come to put in a request. The tone of the discussion maintained this civil air for some time, but when it became obvious this civil request would be denied, Tom threw down his fork, screamed at his father, and walked out. Carl was embarrassed and apologized for his son's behavior. Liz came back with dessert and took up a previous subject of conversation as if nothing had happened.

Soon afterward, I left to look at houses, and because the guest room had its own entrance, let myself in on my return. I was shocked to find Carl sitting on the bed in the dark. He again apologized, but said he had to talk. It was just past ten, and Tom was still gone. Carl was worried. He said that Tom had thrown these fits before and had always returned. His real fear was that his eldest son was turning sour. Tom had a mind of his own, was constantly demanding things, would hold to his demands until he got what he wanted, and, to add insult to injury, his younger brother Jack was now picking up the behavior. I listened for several minutes before he proposed that we go to his den and have a drink.

After we had settled into our armchairs in his well-appointed den, Carl took a long breath and asked me what I thought he and Liz should do. He exhibited all the signs of a father who was honestly hurting, and because of that I agreed to continue the discussion as long as Carl realized I was not qualified to be an individual or family therapist, and that if I were, it would not be ethical to treat a friend. He laughed for the first time that evening and said he knew me too well to take anything I said seriously, but he was in dire need of feedback from a friend he could trust.

With the ground rules set, we decided to free-associate to explore what might be going on in young Tom's mind. I asked Carl if Tom usually got what he wanted. He said not all the time, but most of the time, yes, he got what he wanted. I asked several more questions about Tom's personality traits, and when I had the information I needed to get a handle on just what this boy was like, I started laughing. The father was describing his son, and the son was as I had remembered the father when we were in college together: bullheaded, persistent, and aggressive. Carl had become a successful man because of these traits. Tom was using these same characteristics to get what he wanted.

When I pointed this out, Carl was offended. "I never talked back to my father. I worked hard on the family farm. I earned everything I ever got." Still in his fit of anger, he went on to say that all he needed to do was say no. "That's the trouble with this generation. Kids today are spoiled. Parents don't know how to say no and mean it." I agreed that saying no and meaning it is important, but Tom had long since gone beyond the point where a simple "No" would have any real impact.

It was then that I began to understand the key point so many of us miss when we try to control the problem of overindulgence: In many cases, our children are no longer children. They are like freight trains that have gained momentum, and we have no method of putting on the brakes. But our attempts at control are dominated by a belief that they are still children. Fifteen-year-old Tom was shaving, undoubtedly had pubic hair, and was beginning to show other definite signs of maturity and independence.

In many cultures there is some type of ceremony, like the bar mitzvah, that marks a child's entry into adulthood. With this entry into adulthood comes the expectation of change. They are to put away their toys and begin to adopt the behavior of adulthood. But for many children there is no such occasion, and unless children grow up on a farm, where the necessity of sharing work allows them a graceful entry into adulthood, they end up being adults whose only responsibilities are making the bed and taking out the garbage, if that.

At some point Carl needed to tell his son that he was now an adult and it was time he started behaving like one. Carl and Liz needed to develop a ceremony that would help Tom realize that there is great joy in getting things you have wanted and worked hard for. In a few short years they were going to expect their almost sixteen-year-old son to go into the world and function as a man. The family was distracted by Tom's demands. Tom was misdirecting his need for independence, his need for respect as an adult, his need to accomplish.

Helping your child to realize he is becoming an adult

cannot be accomplished in one intense confrontation or a ceremony. A ceremony is useful only because it designates a specific age at which parent and child are encouraged to recognize the inevitability of adulthood.

In this instance I am talking about the need to set some new ground rules in the relationship with your almost grown child who is still acting like a spoiled brat. How do the Carls of the world convince the Toms of the world that it is time to dispense with childish demands and take on the self-discipline and responsibilities of adulthood?

We can start by setting an age, a birthday, when new expectations take effect. Sixteen seems to be the popular choice. At sixteen your children get that all-important document that says they now have the right to use the car or have a car of their own. The driver's license forces most parents to set some new guidelines, and that's not a bad idea. The car brings up issues of independence, responsibility, and money management. Why not tell them: Yes, you can use the car, but with this adult privilege comes specific responsibilities. The insurance costs money, and with a sixteen-year-old on the policy the premium skyrockets. That portion can be paid by the teenager. And when your teenager says, "But I don't have any money, or a job," you then have the opportunity to explain the need for them to go into the world of work and learn how to compete. The insurance also allows you to explain the effect of accidents and traffic tickets on next year's premium.

Your child may know that you can afford to purchase him a new vehicle and pay the insurance, but this is the time to explain what you will pay for and what you won't. You are asking him to take on this responsibility because he must learn how to care for himself. It is time for him to acquire the discipline to save for things he cannot afford now.

Several issues come into play with this crossing into adulthood. I have talked about the change we expect of children, but parents must change as well. You can expect them to assume more responsibility, but at the same time, mothers and fathers have to begin to see their daughters and sons as adults. With these responsibilities come freedoms. Increased privileges must be given by the parent. It's not enough to pretend they are becoming adults. They are.

You need to think about how you talk to them and what you say. Have you ever considered taking your sixteen-year-old into your confidence, and discussing that problem you're having at work. Admit you're too close to the situation and need advice from someone with some objectivity. When I was seventeen my grandfather was ill, and my father turned to me and asked what I thought we should do regarding the future. For Dad it was a casual question, and I doubt he remembers doing it, but for me, that seventeen-year-old boy/man, it was an emotional benchmark. I was proud that Dad wanted my advice, and at the same time, I was forced to think about the seriousness inherent in adult decisions.

You need to consult them regarding their future. What do they want to do with their lives? If they want college, sixteen is almost too late to begin the planning. If they want a trade, you need to think of trade schools or union affiliations. Obviously, you can discuss these issues at any age, but this is a perfect time to use the discussion of their future to impress upon them the gravity of these new expectations.

We spoil our kids because we love them, but it's a selfish love if we send them into the world unprepared.

3

Good parents provide structure.

I was conferring with the director of the Menninger Youth Program in Atlanta the night before a training session when the quality of her family-care parents came up. I asked whether she could rank the couples in order of effectiveness. The program in Atlanta was new but she was confident that she could provide such a ranking. She laughed as she said that it would be impossible for me to identify the good from the bad by looking at them, and she doubted that the training session would provide clues to their relative value in the homes. I asked her to write the

names in order, from best to worst, to put the list somewhere safe, and not to show it to me until I had made my
own list.

On the next evening, after the first day of training, we
met again and I brought out my list. The director was
shocked to discover that it was identical to hers. As much
as I would like to claim superior knowledge and extrasen-
sory perception, neither is the case. She was right when
she insinuated that no one, professional or otherwise, can
pick out quality parents through short-term observation
or by evaluating their personal histories. I was able to
make the correct rating using a very simple exercise that I
conducted soon after introductions were made on the first
morning of training. Each set of parents was asked to go to
a section of the blackboard and list a typical weekday and
weekend schedule in their respective homes. We know
from hard-won experience that the parents who provide
the appropriate structure in their home have the happiest,
most secure children. Secure children do not act out, run
away, fight, or resist authority as much as those who never
know the rules or what might happen next.

At the blackboard one father stood with chalk in hand,
not quite sure where to begin, and his wife was unable to
prompt a thought. I put their names on the bottom of my
list two minutes into the exercise. The couple who began
to write immediately and to list confidently the day's activities, from breakfast to bedtime, went to the top of my
list.

Structure is the glue that holds any good human endeavor together. But do not confuse structure with rigidity. One has nothing to do with the other. Structure is the

key to successful business and homes. Rigidity destroys and confuses.

When appropriate limits and schedules are imposed, children are given their first lessons in understanding how to live in our complicated society. Through structure children learn law. Law is not learned in law schools or at police stations. Our understanding of the rules that govern our social order are learned at home from parents who know how to set appropriate limits and how to assign certain tasks that help a child realize his role as a responsible member of a group.

Somehow we associate structure with punishment when, in fact, that is clearly not the case, structure provides security and freedom. Children feel lost when they do not know what the limits are, even though they constantly test these limits. We see this most in adolescents when they not only test the boundaries but, in some cases, step over the rules and challenge us as they seek independence. This age-old process is their way of saying that they are individuals in their own right, and the ritual, painful as it may be for all concerned, is an essential part of growing up. During this tumultuous period, it is tempting to give in and ignore the rules on which children depend as they grow up. This tug of war lasts until they are truly independent, but if they pull and there is no resistance, the adolescent can and often does fall.

I was listening to a program on the radio in which a great jazz musician was being interviewed. The local disc jockey conducting the interview was trying very hard to sound like an expert and said something about the total freedom associated with the music. The old musician laughed and said, "The best jazz has a structure that allows individual freedom." The analogy struck a responsive chord in me. I have always believed that when there is a definite pattern of rules within a family, it allows more freedom for the individual members. To carry the comparison one step further, families that adopt and live within a caring structure are comforted by the compatible rhythms associated with their everyday routine. These routines enable the individuals within the family to function without being overwhelmed by moment-to-moment decisions. It's easy to become paralyzed by minutiae. As with many valued possessions, however, we seldom appreciate or acknowledge the existence of structure until we lose it.

I travel extensively and have learned like the turtle to carry with me some movable patterns of behavior. When I began traveling, however, the loss of my usual day-to-day schedule of events was devastating. I would get off the plane, go to the hotel room, and be left with six hours of time to kill before bedtime. Work did not begin until the next day, I was too tired to be productive, the book I had picked up at the airport stank, and I didn't like anything on television that night. Did I lie down; did I go for a walk; what time did I go to bed? I was talking about this with my daughter Lisa when she moved into her first apartment. She was excited about the freedom, but after the furniture was in place and the dishes put away, she too felt empty and didn't know what to do with herself. The best way to appreciate the routines that guide everyday behavior is to lose them.

In Chapter 2, I introduced J.J. and John Heart and Lewis P., the irascible delinquent. J.J. was the primary care parent in one of the first group homes I had created and was an expert on structure. When the defiant teenager

Lewis P. came into her home, he had only had experience living in detention homes, jails, and, for seven months, in a reform school. Lewis thought he knew more about structure than anyone in the house. In the reform school, every minute of every day was scheduled, but in fact Lewis was confusing rigid discipline with structure. The major difference is that people who are rigid do not consider individual needs, whereas structure is a shared experience created for everyone's benefit.

Remember that when Lewis P. moved into the house, J.J. allowed him a grace period before she began to insist on his participation in the ways of the Heart household. As he sat back and watched the people living together, he was frankly confused by the happy countenance of the children. Returning to a pattern of behavior that he was comfortable with, he tried to come between the other residents and the Hearts. What he in fact did was tell the boys in the house that they were wimps. If they had any guts they would not jump every time J.J. asked them to do something. The children, many of whom had gone through the same process Lewis was now experiencing, simply laughed at him. Some of them tried to tell him he could trust the Hearts. Like most new residents, Lewis was more susceptible to suggestions from the other children than from the adults, but he was not about to buy in quickly.

The day Lewis graduated from high school I sat up with him half the night talking about his life in this new and strange environment. The one issue that kept popping up as he tried to define his transformation was the structure they all lived by. Lewis described it as "J.J.'s way." He said, "It's like a living thing that just keeps pulling you in." He described the smell of bacon frying every morning and how it would pull him out of bed. Lewis hated sitting down to breakfast, and for the first two or three months, he would sit staring at the food and glaring at the other residents. While J.J. kept fixing breakfast, John would roll Lewis out of bed, tell him to clean his room, make his bed, take a shower, and come to breakfast.

Lewis threw on his clothes and ignored the rest of the instructions. "They just kept doing the same things, over and over and over. And when I would want some of the special freedoms that the other kids got, John and J.J. would remind me that I had not made my bed, or taken a shower, or done my homework, and the privileges came with some strings. They didn't get mad, and when they told me I couldn't do something, they seemed to be honestly sorry, but they stuck with it, and there were many times it would have been much easier to let me have my way. I was a real asshole, but they stuck with me."

As you read this, you must be wondering why Lewis was resisting, and at the same time asking yourself why your child resists your fair and useful guidance. Lewis was resisting because the structure was not fun, and this could very easily be the same reason your child would give. He had never experienced schedules, limits, and the notion that if you wanted something you had to work for it. Lewis got what he wanted through brute force, and saw no reason to develop skills or consider other options. "That first month, the only thing that kept me from running was the threat of being taken back to the reform school. But I stayed, and pretty soon old J.J. and John wore me down. I started by eating some bacon."

The notion that kids do not *like* structure and responsibility is not new. If your children are normal, they will resist. I have had parents ask how you make homework, household chores, or bedtime fun, and my answer is that you don't. It doesn't have to be fun. In spite of advertisements to the contrary, all of life is not fun. It can be rewarding and enriching, but the fact remains that parents must instill a sense of structure and self-discipline if their children are going to be successful adults. I do not like to go to work every day, but I usually end up feeling pretty good about being there. I do not like to cut the lawn or paint the house, but there is a real sense of pride when I see the trimmed yard or painted wood. We all know people who promise to do something but never follow through. They are usually not happy or successful adults and keep wondering why no one respects them.

Teaching your child to live by and appreciate structures requires that you be structured. Preaching *at* your children can be equated to spitting into the wind: It's pretty messy and has very little effect.

I have found that in successful homes the basic rules are very similar. The methods of enforcement are as varied as the number of people involved, but the basic framework is the same. The following important routines may not be wildly innovative, but they are the basics that all of us need to be reminded of.

A good way to begin is to get up and fix breakfast. This issue was clearly illustrated one spring day when I was working with a young set of family-care parents. They were eager and dedicated, but their home was chaotic. We were trying to come up with some understanding of the problem when I asked how they got the kids out of bed. She said they set their alarms, put the cereal out the night before, and yelled at them twice. If they didn't get up, they were put on restriction. As it turned out they yelled at them from their bed. When I asked why they didn't get up and fix a hot breakfast, they said they were exhausted. Everyone in the house stayed up late, talking and playing games, and they were tired in the morning.

Getting up and going to bed mark the beginning and end of each day, and how it is or is not managed will often influence one's attitude toward other events throughout the day. For children, the only thing harder than going to bed is getting up. It is important for them to get up and get moving. Many of the children we work with are depressed, and one of the symptoms is a resistance to getting out of bed in the morning. They lie brooding under the protection of the covers and the longer they linger, the more depressed they get. It is possible for the same thing to happen to your children. People feel better when they learn to wake up and get up.

I keep repeating this notion of preparing a *hot* breakfast, but believe it or not I do not have a fixation on the temperature of food in the morning. I recommend a hot meal to emphasize the value of a set event. Breakfast then becomes associated with the smells of coffee, bacon, eggs, pancakes, or hot cereal. Just as the smell of bacon was a strong influence on Lewis P.'s eventual change in behavior, your child will soon begin to identify these smells and the event in a positive way. She will also get a nutritional kick before she goes out to learn or play hard. The effort you make in the preparation itself says you care.

Equal emphasis should be placed on a sit-down dinner. The very act of expecting the family to be at the same place at the same time is important. Dinner provides an opportunity share your thoughts. An English psychiatrist came to the United States to look at our Menninger family-care homes and was amazed at the compatibility of the individuals in our family groups. It could be said that our family-care homes resemble the United Nations Assembly because many races, creeds, and age groups are placed in each home. He asked J. J. Heart if her family participated in a formal group therapy session. She said, "Sure we do, but we call it dinnertime." Dinnertime is the time to communicate and to work on family issues. Evening activities begin after dinner, and parents can monitor those activities better if the hour set for this meal is considered sacred by all participants.

Personal hygiene should also be part of your child's everyday routine. Parents may feel like recording such phrases as "brush your teeth," "wash your hands," "comb your hair," and "take your shower" so that when a particular instruction was needed, they could simply push a button. But no matter how frustrating it may be, you need to repeat those phrases over and over again. (On those rare occasions when your children follow the instructions and you look at the mess they left in their wake, you may wonder why you insisted.)

These chores will be completed with fewer reminders if you hold out the expectation that they may be accomplished within the same time frame every day. It is best not to wait until the young person who looks like a pigpen is ready to walk out the door to a waiting school bus before you confront the fact that his or her hair, hands, teeth, and face are dirty. J.J. would stand next to the table laden with her hearty breakfast and inspect the kids as they came down to eat. At the same time John would inspect the rooms to make sure that the clothes were picked up and the beds made. If one of the assigned tasks was not completed, the children were expected to do it in the evening during their free time. It did not take the children long to begin to follow through on their own. Room maintenance and personal cleanliness became second nature when the expectation was there day in and day out.

Homework should never be considered in the realm of optional activities. Some children do it on their own and never need reminding, but the vast majority resist books with a dedication akin to fanaticism, and the only cure is a scheduled, supervised study period.

Have you ever heard these words coming from your child: "But I don't have any homework. Are you going to make me sit here and suffer while every other kid in the world is out playing?"

Over the years I have found that most of the children in our programs have come to us two and three years behind their age group in school. Many were fifteen- and sixteen-year-olds who could not read. In most cases, this was the direct result of social deprivation. But the future employer wanting a worker capable of accomplishing a task will not care why the applicant cannot read or follow instructions. As a result, schoolwork takes on new dimensions, and we let the children know what it means to their future.

In our project, we start by accepting the fact that they need to learn how to study and let the school know that in the beginning we want a daily report on their behavior and accomplishments. We have devised a form that the child takes to school. The form is filled out and signed by the teacher. It's a checklist that tells us how they are functioning and leaves a space for assigned homework.

If your child is coming home with no homework, but getting failing grades, I would suggest you develop a form of your own and start a structured study time. If he needs special help that you can't provide, hire a tutor. If you can't afford a tutor, talk to your child's teachers or school officials. You may be amazed at the cooperative response. Most educators I know are dedicated people and will do back flips for parents trying to advance their child's learning skills. Your child needs to know that you and the school are working together to give her the best possible start. If you don't get cooperation, go to a school board meeting and raise hell. There are books filled with statistics proving that your child's future is dependent upon the quality of the education she receives.

A recent "Sixty Minutes" segment focused on the disproportionate number of oriental students getting the best academic scholarships at the most prestigious universities. Mike Wallace did not have to use many of his investigative skills to discover that the children were coming from homes where the parents expected them to study and achieve in school. Throughout the interview, Mike Wallace kept asking the students about the effect of this kind of pressure and whether they were being damaged by their parents' drive for them to succeed. Most of them laughed and said it was just a part of being born into that particular household. They also considered academic achievement a challenge and looked forward to the competition.

I am not suggesting you structure every minute of every day, but I am suggesting that you set some priorities and let your children know by the emphasis you place on those activities what you consider important.

Most good and caring parents I have known over the
years initiated a study time for those children who were
having trouble in school and allowed the others to manage
their homework as needed. John and J. J. Heart kept the
study hour in place for everyone, regardless of their
grades or accomplishments. When the kids would complain, she would say that one of the greatest gifts given by
God was the ability to learn, and when they learned for
their own sake and not the school's, she would consider
giving up the study hour.

Before I begin to make J. J. Heart sound like the captain
of a slave ship, let me assure you that she was as good at
bending the rules as she was in making them. One night
Lewis P. told me of the occasions when, right in the middle of study hour, J.J. would sing for everyone to stop
what they were doing and run to the van. She was having
a sweet attack and needed to rush immediately to the
Dairy Queen for a transfusion. No one ever knew when
the ice cream alarm would sound, but it was awaited with
giddy anticipation. One Friday evening the children came
home from school to find a rented bus sitting in the front
drive. John informed them that they had forty minutes to
pack their bags for a week-long field trip to Colorado.
They missed five days of school, but Lewis said he learned
more that week than any week he had spent in school. As
Lewis was talking, some of the other children in the house
told of the days they woke up feeling down and how J.J.
would suggest they skip school to stay home and help her
around the house. In spite of her structure, living with J.J.
was a constant adventure, *and the rules were designed to benefit the people living under that roof, not just to preserve order.*

In any discussion of family structure, it would be delinquent of me to ignore the house we live in. If you look up the word structure in the dictionary, you will discover that the first definition listed deals with building and construction. Our home is our castle and represents many things, among them security and self-image. If a child grows up in a house with holes in the walls, dirt on the floors, and paint peeling from the siding, his sense of self is affected accordingly.

The Menninger family-care concept was born twenty-five years ago when a group of us began to comprehend the frightening statistics coming from the foster home placement records. Children were being pushed from one placement to another at an alarming rate. When we asked them why they were uncomfortable, why they felt bad in the foster home, their response was universal: "It was *their* bed, *their* dog, *their* food, *their* house, I was always a visitor."

Like most people they did not like to be constantly given to. They were perpetual guests and, as such, second-class members of the family. We all want our own things and a place of our own. When we would talk to these children immediately upon their return to detention homes and other assorted holding facilities, it was impossible not to notice the sack they carried with them. It wasn't always a sack; sometimes it was an old suitcase or pillowcase, but the contents were generally the same. It included old alarm clocks that didn't work, wrinkled and torn family photographs, teddy bears with no stuffing. It was junk, but it was *their* junk, and they would have fought hard to keep it.

When I began to consider alternative care systems that would address these crucial issues, I knew that the houses our kids would live in would be theirs. After they are accepted into our program, we bring them to the house and say, "This is your house. We have bought it for you. You will be sharing it with other children and a set of family-care parents, but this is your house, and this is your bed, your dresser, and your closet." It is psychologically important for children to have a *place* they call home. Not long ago we brought an enterprising young man into one of the houses in our project. We told him that the bed was his, and he went out and sold it!

The care and use of the house within our project is an important part of a child's sense of structure. We have learned from experience that the maintenance of the building we call home is one important key to the way the people within it function. When the children move in, the house is either new or completely renovated. The walls are clean, the floor coverings stain free, and the appliances in working order, and we expect it to be kept that way. The children participate in the maintenance, just as your child should participate in the care and cleaning of your home. These chores should be started at an early age. Cleaning is not a mother's job, and painting is not the father's job. Everyone who lives in the house is responsible for her fair share of the duties. If you drop it, pick it up; if you dirty it, clean it up; and if it doesn't work, fix it.

While I was working on this particular section of the book, I noticed that my two-year-old son was intentionally throwing food from his high chair onto the floor. Realizing that I was self-righteously telling parents everywhere that it is never too early to get your kids involved in the cleaning and upkeep, I told Nicholas that he was too old to throw food, and that when we were finished eating he would have to pick up everything he had thrown down. Nicholas told me to buy a dog. I don't know where the idea came from, but I suspect my wife's sister Terry told him to say that.

The structure and makeup of the community in which you live can influence your child. If you live in a neighborhood where most of the individuals residing in it are stable, well-adjusted people and your child's peers are confident and outgoing, your child will identify with them. I went to my daughter's high school to take her the gym shoes she had forgotten. While I was waiting for her, I overheard a group of teenagers talking around a locker. They were discussing what they wanted to do when they got out of school. It was not an issue of what they *could* do but rather what they *wanted* to do. They were confident that they could achieve almost any goal in life, and most of them have achieved accordingly. I am not suggesting that successful parents must be rich, but you need to think seriously about where you live, and the impact of the area on your children.

I was in Chicago twenty years ago raising funds to start one of our first projects for abandoned, abused, and otherwise displaced children. I was telling a potential contributor how much our homes would cost, and the fact that they would be located in upper-middle-class neighborhoods. She was surprised, and commented that since many of our children came from poverty-stricken environments, they would be spoiled in our houses and would no longer be comfortable returning to the ghettos. I told her that I sure as hell hoped they would be uncomfortable returning to poverty and that we would do everything within our power to increase that discomfort. Living in middle-class homes in middle-class neighborhoods does have an impact. For the first time many of our children begin to believe that they can make it in affluent society. They realize that those hoity-toity people who seem to have so many unattainable things are not too different from themselves. In this case, exposure breeds confidence.

When a parent provides appropriate guidelines a child will begin to develop *self*-discipline. Later in this book, I deal more extensively with issues of discipline, but I cannot overemphasize the importance of structure as it affects the development of self-discipline, which is the ultimate goal of every parent.

Parents who provide structure may hear a lot of complaints but are loved the most in the end. Their children are prepared to achieve in a competitive world.

4

Good parents get to know their child by becoming actively involved in his interests.

"I didn't know—I just didn't know." If there is one catch-phrase that I hear more than others, it would be "I didn't know."

This past year I sat with the parents of a seventeen-year-old boy who had just been convicted of possessing and selling cocaine. He was a senior in high school, was popular with his peers, and had not been a problem at home. According to his father, Andrew was quiet and "took care of himself." Somehow it seemed very important to the father that Andrew was able to take care of himself. When asked what else they knew about Andrew, the mother and father looked at each other, confused by the question. His mother said that they owned their own business and both of them worked hard to give Andrew the things they did not have when they were growing up.

These two intelligent, caring parents did not know that their son was addicted to alcohol and cocaine, and had been for three years; that their son was introduced to drugs by the young couple who lived next door; that this same couple would spend the night in their home when they went on trips; or that their son was functionally illiterate and cried when he talked to me about his school experience.

This young man dropped clues everywhere, but only in retrospect did his parents hear his desperate pleas for help. When he came home late from school, he went directly to bed and slept well into the evening. His eyes were often bloodshot and his pupils dilated. In the early stages of his habit, Andrew was constantly in need of extra money and used wild, unreasonable excuses to justify the expense. Later on, when other kids started calling him at all hours of the day and night, the need for cash vanished. He told them he hated school, but neither his mother nor his father pursued the issue.

Andrew was tried as an adult, and in prison they discovered that he had an IQ of 136 and was suffering from dyslexia. He could not read. When his father was told this, he doubled his fist, pounded the desk, and screamed obscenities at the school system which his taxes supported.

The father's reaction was typical. He really believed that it was the school's responsibility to educate his child. But in fact it was not just the school's responsibility—it was also his. Parents are responsible for their youngster's education. The school can be a grand and rich resource, but it is up to the parents to know their children and their needs.

Much of my knowledge has come from my exposure to parents who have failed, leaving the state to assume the responsibility for the care and feeding of the child. In most of the cases I deal with, the individual members of the family simply do not know each other. They occasionally eat together, open presents together, and grunt at each other when they get up in the morning, but when it comes to real knowledge and insight, they live in their own worlds. When I ask them what activities they participate in together, I usually get blank looks.

Unlike the sea turtle that lays its eggs far from the water's edge and then leaves its offspring to find their own way in life, the human animal requires nurturance, support, guidance, and love in the process of growing up. Humans simply do not raise themselves successfully.

Unfortunately, we sometimes mistakenly conceive of the school system, day-care centers, city recreation departments, and "Sesame Street" as surrogate parents. Once our kids get to be old enough to go to school or to participate in supervised group activities, it is all too easy for parents to get distracted and to relinquish the care of their children to others. When this happens the family can stop functioning as an effective unit. We can forget that we must *stay* involved, that parenting is a continuing process.

When I suggest that you get involved with your children, I recognize that many families will need to start by getting to know each other. Soon after I developed one of the first projects, which included five separate group homes, I realized that we had a house that was not working. All the elements for success were in place. The family-care parents were skilled and caring. The six children were no more difficult or disturbed than those living in the other homes in our various projects. Yet somehow the process of bonding that we expect to see after the first six months was not taking place. Like all families in which the members function as individuals, as opposed to a cohesive group, the pressure was beginning to build. Small problems were viewed as major disasters. Everyone's weaknesses and fears were exaggerated and exposed.

After several team meetings and consultations with our professional staff, the father in the home came up with a ridiculous idea. He wanted to load up, six kids and all, and go on a backpacking trip. I laughed, but I was also unable to suggest a better solution. After two weeks in the Rocky Mountains, eight people—four boys, two girls, and a very happy set of family-care parents—became a family. When you stop and think about it, the logic is elementary: They were alone in a new environment and had to depend on each other to survive. Without television, radios, or telephones the group learned to communicate, to begin functioning as a team.

Take a vacation together. It doesn't have to be a backpacking trip, but you do need to get away from the distractions of business, friends, and telephones. Before you can know your children, you need to get involved, and through shared activities you will begin to understand how they think and what they dream. You may even end up with some family traditions.

Successful families, surrogate and biological, create a bond that is stronger than those found in other groups.

This simplistic realization was dramatically illustrated to me twenty-five years ago when I began to look at the alternative care systems for children who have been removed from abusive homes. At the time I was trying to understand why so many of the neglected children placed in the foster care system failed. The kids referred to us by the court were not that tough to care for, and the foster families that I had met were well meaning and sincere in their desire to provide appropriate care. If all of this was true, why were children being rejected at a phenomenal rate? The average length of stay of a child in one foster home was three months, and I would guess that the same is true today.

When I began to research the issue, several obvious truths began to surface, which have been invaluable to us as we created our existing family-care home concept. What I discovered is that the secure family is perhaps the most complicated social structure in our society. The rules that allow a family to function as a group are unwritten and in most cases unconscious. These rules are not posted on the refrigerator door, and if you asked any individual to list the regulations that existed in his family, he would laugh and say they don't have any. The best way to become aware of their existence is to have some dear friends come to visit you in your home for a week. The very same friends who share most of your deepest values and beliefs soon become a first-class pain in the ass. They leave the lid to the toilet seat up, let the dog out the front door, squeeze the toothpaste backward, leave the milk out, and so on. These outsiders stomp all over the rules you did not think about before their arrival.

Eighty percent of all communication in a close family is

nonverbal. Researchers find that there is an extraordinarily detailed vocabulary of facial expressions. Paul Ekman of the University of California at San Francisco and other scholars have determined that the facial muscles permit more than a thousand different facial signals. I can determine how my wife, Ginger, feels when she walks down the stairs in the morning just by the way she walks. If she is not feeling well, I can see it and respond accordingly. This is a language that an outsider would not understand. Strangers to the family simply do not know what you are thinking.

The foster child comes from a very different world. He is frightened and sensitive to every mood change and soon realizes that he is not a part of this group. Unknowingly, he stomps all over the rules and is unable to understand 80 percent of the communication. Because he doesn't comprehend the language, he makes major mistakes. The outsider becomes a constant irritant. This child, not unlike a heart transplanted into another human body, is soon rejected. Everyone, including the family doing the rejecting, is hurt and angered by the experience. The child leaves, convinced that he or she is bad and deserving of the rejection, and the family is guilt-ridden but usually becomes defensive to cover the guilt. I am convinced that the foster home concept can and often does fail *because* of the strength of the family. Good families become encapsulated units that provide security for those within. This ends up being a catch-22. The stray child needs a secure home, but the secure home has the natural tendency to reject outsiders.

From these observations, I began to understand how successful families function. There is a bond, but this bond is not created by blood, it is created through shared experiences.

When Carl, my old college friend, sat down to have a heart-to-heart talk with his fifteen-year-old son, Tom, he discovered a terrible thing. He didn't know his son, and his son didn't know him. Carl knew Tom's taste in music, his grades, and the names of his friends, but he didn't know what Tom liked, or feared, or wanted out of life. When he tried to have a meaningful conversation in response to Tom's constant demands for things like the motorbike, the communication broke down immediately.

As Carl described this event several months later, he was amazed at his own ignorance, and instinctively knew that something dramatic needed to take place to effect change. On the night we talked about his concerns for his son, I had told him about the family-care parents who took a backpacking trip in the mountains. In Chapter 2, I left the story of Carl and Tom at the point where they were trying to communicate. After two failed attempts, this desperate father, remembering the backpacking trip, put his son in the car, told his wife they would be back in a few days, and drove off into the night. Carl had no destination in mind but was determined to get acquainted with the adolescent stranger who was living in his house. The thing that shocked this father most was the embarrassment they both felt as they began to reach out to each other.

At the outset they didn't discuss serious issues or probe for deep feelings, they simply talked. Tom asked his father what kind of work he did, and how many people worked for him. Carl was somewhat relieved when I told him that one of the hardest questions for college freshmen to answer on their entrance applications was the description of their parents' professions. Carl asked Tom what he wanted to do when he got out of college and discovered Tom didn't want to go to college. He loved cars, motorbikes, and any other vehicle that had a motor in it. He wanted to be a mechanic, and has since become one. Carl and his son got to know each other, and even to like each other; from that point on Carl and Liz began to get involved and to work at the relationship they had with their sons.

I keep talking about vacations and driving off into the night. These are dramatic events that can be useful in breaking the ice, but they are certainly not the answer to the everyday maintenance of a parent-child relationship. When we think about relationships with our children, we immediately conjure up a structured or manufactured activity. The best way to get involved is to include them in your everyday life. Take them to work, explain to them what you do, and introduce them to your colleagues. These people are important to you, and your child needs to put faces with the names you bring up over the dinner table.

When you go to the store or the bank, take your children with you. As a child, my oldest son, Michael, was the most prolific question asker I have ever encountered. He is now a freelance editor and does work for groups such as the National Academy of Sciences. His knowledge and skill amaze me, but when he was three and four I was the expert, and he would go everywhere I went in the car. A typical exchange between us sounded like this:

"What's that?"

"That's a bank."

"What does a bank do?"

"You put money in it."

"Why do you put money in it?"

"Because they keep it safe for us, and we can get it when we want it."

"Why do they need to keep it safe? Is somebody going to rob us?"

By the time we got home from these sojourns into the community, Michael had learned something, and in most cases I had some new insight into his feelings. On that particular trip we ended up talking about people who rob and steal, and other things that go bump in the night. He told me how he would lie very still so the bad people would not know he was there. During our rides together we talked about things that would not have been exposed without my involvement. There were times when we said nothing but the opportunity was there, and through exposure he knew me well enough to broach *almost* any subject. Note that I have emphasized almost. We will never know, nor should we know, everything our children are thinking. They need their private thoughts as much as we need ours.

I have a friend, Bert, who is a dedicated jogger. He told me that every time he puts on his shoes and shorts, his three-year-old daughter starts to cry; she knows he is going to leave and she wants to come along. Bert was feeling guilty and wanted to know if he should give up jogging. I was adamant when I said no, but I suggested he consider ways to include her in the activity. They now warm up together, stretching the muscles, grunting in unison, touching their toes, and rolling their heads. He bought her some running shoes, and they jog together for a block before he takes off on his own. They don't talk much, but the time together is quality time, and she looks forward to being with her father when he is doing something he loves.

When Bert was describing this experience he used the term tradition. He said their morning jog was becoming "a real tradition." Children love to create traditions, and when you do something more than once and they begin to expect the event to happen again, you have a family tradition. Traditions are comforting and a source of security.

There can also be moments in the lives of your children that are virtually sacred to them, but of which you remain unaware. I was visiting my daughter Lisa, who now lives in Arizona, and we started talking about the barbecues in our backyard. She said she loved those occasions because I gave her the job of squirting out the grease fire with the water gun. It was the one time we were alone together and we could talk. It never occurred to me that those moments in the backyard were important to Lisa, or that we didn't have other regular occasions when we communicated. But as I thought back to special moments with my daughter, my reminiscences did have me standing by the grill.

I remembered best the discussion the day after Lisa was elected homecoming queen. As it turned out I seemed to be more excited about the honor than she was. When I asked her how she felt about it, she shrugged and said that she was relieved. She explained that when you are elected homecoming queen, you are automatically barred from competing for any of the other queen awards. She was now out of the running and freed from the competition. She told me how her friends had betrayed her because of their disappointment. She cried and I held her. I didn't have any grand or healing advice, but we were together and shared the hurt. Lisa was living under pressures I knew nothing about, but I am thankful that we were close enough that she could tell me and that an old water gun and a barbecue pit helped pave the way.

Insight into the inner workings of your child's mind is not a right granted in exchange for paying the bills, and a passive presence in the house does not qualify you as an individual worthy of confidences. You need to become active and involved.

Call the school and find out how your children are functioning in each class. Don't wait for the teacher's conference. Let them know you want to be kept up to date on every aspect of your child's education. They will welcome your concern. How many times have you asked, "How was school today?" and received the reply, "Fine!" If you know what is going on, you can ask specific questions and you may be surprised when you get detailed answers. I also suggest you allow your child some time to decompress and relax after school before you start a conversation. School is hard work, and, like you, they may come home ready to kick the dog.

Find something you enjoy doing together. If you do not want to lead a scout troop or coach a team, don't. Your child is not stupid and is very sensitive to your moods. If you are trying to give in spite of your discomfort, you will both be miserable. Search for an activity that is mutually satisfying. Your child does not want to be around you when you are a grump. Think about how often you include your child when you are doing something you love.

Know who their friends are. Many parents have denied being responsible for their child's problems and say outside influences were the cause of his criminal behavior. Find out what those outside influences are and direct change. All too often we attempt to direct change by passing judgment and giving lectures. If your children are secure enough in their relationship with you to expose insecurities, they just might admit that bad friends are the only friends they can find. Direct change by helping them find new, positive interests that will replace their need to maintain negative involvements.

If you don't know what your child is interested in, say so. Confess your ignorance, and keep probing until you get some answers. Once these secret dreams are exposed, do whatever you can to make them come true. If he likes cars, get an old one and let him work on it. Get him involved in a club that rebuilds antique cars. If she likes skiing, help her join the local ski club, and borrow the money if you need to make a commitment to encourage her to go on that trip three months later, or match whatever money she saves. Do what you can to encourage them to get involved with new friends through these activities that will expose them to new friends. Parents who behave like helpless victims are contributing to their child's downfall.

Obviously, the opposite extreme is the parent who lives vicariously through his children and has little or no life of his own. This is almost as destructive as no interaction. Quite frankly, however, I cannot think of a case in which the overinvolvement resulted in tragedy.

I began this chapter discussing the young high school senior who was committed to the state prison for selling cocaine. He is now developing a relationship with his parents. It is never too late.

5

Good parents work hard to communicate with their children.

Before I was the director of juvenile court services I served my apprenticeship as a probation officer in a large Midwestern city. It was an exciting time in my life. I had just finished some graduate courses that had stimulated me as no previous educational experience had and for the first time I felt confident in the direction of my career. With the boldness of youth, newfound knowledge, and a sense of purpose, I charged in to save whatever portion of the world I could get hold of. I have never been smarter, before or since I started that job. I went into that court the expert's expert.

The judge must have been keeping his eye out for an expert's expert, because he gave me a special assignment. Now that I think back on the experience, I can see the mischievous twinkle in his eye, but at the time I thought it was pure joy at having found a young man capable of solving his problem cases. The other probation officers were carrying caseloads of between forty and fifty juveniles. I was given nineteen, but these were the problem cases, the worst of the worst. In each instance, the judge would issue each of these young adults a final warning before commitment to the state reform school and would then turn the case over to me. One more violation and off they would go. Each of these nineteen boys had gone through an extensive probation experience, but were continuing to get into trouble.

At the time, I was more than confident that I was the man for the job. I was convinced that all I would have to do was sit down and talk to these young criminals about the error of their ways. I would communicate with them. I would tell them that it is stupid to choose crime as a profession. Criminals eventually get caught, and spend most of their lives in miserable, dark, dirty prisons.

Of my nineteen cases, Oliver was the one I liked best. Most of the others were unresponsive, angry teenagers who would stare at their feet, pick their fingernails, or sneer with a disgusted curl of the upper lip as I tried to talk with them. But Oliver was different. He smiled and looked you in the face when he shook hands, and he laughed at my jokes.

Oliver stole cars. At the age of seventeen, he had the honor of having stolen more cars than any criminal, adult or child, in the city that particular year. I always wondered if he had confessed to crimes he had not committed in order to help the police clean up their unsolved car theft cases. Regardless, Oliver did steal cars.

One day we decided to go outside for a walk instead of sitting in my hot, stuffy office. As we strolled down the street I began to notice that Oliver had a twitch. His head would jerk right and then down. Finally I asked him how long he had lived with this nervous condition. When he understood what I was talking about, he started laughing. It wasn't a twitch, he was looking for keys in the ignitions of the parked cars that we passed next to the sidewalk. Oliver said it was an old habit that he would have to rid himself of, now that I had convinced him that stealing cars was stupid. Even in those days of my enthusiastic naïveté, I was savvy enough to realize that Oliver did at times put me on.

After we got to know each other and he was more comfortable with me, he began to test the relationship by showing up late for his probation appointment. It kept getting worse and worse, until he was missing half and three quarters of his hour. I had warned him several times, and finally gave him an ultimatum. Show up for the next appointment on time or he was going back before the judge. On the next Wednesday, Oliver walked in the door two minutes early. I was proud of him and told him so. Five minutes later the police walked in and arrested him. Oliver had stolen a car to get to his probation appointment on time. He would have gotten away with it, but he parked next to a fire hydrant directly in front of the entrance of the juvenile court building.

I personally took him to be checked into the detention center, which was two floors up in the same building. He didn't appear to be upset, and when I asked him why he did it, he looked at me with a quizzical expression and said, "Stealing cars is what I do."

I told him I would go to his home to notify his mother rather than use the phone. Oliver looked confused, shrugged, and said, "Whatever." It honestly didn't seem to make any difference to him how his mother was told, and I soon learned why. He lived in an old apartment house six blocks from the juvenile court building. When I got there no one would answer the buzzer in the lobby, but it was a hot summer day and most of the residents were sitting out on little balconies in the front of the five-story building.

I looked up and recognized Mrs. P. three floors up. I yelled that we needed to talk. She asked what I wanted. I said we should talk in private, it concerned her son, Oliver. She said these were her friends and I could say what I wanted to say. By this time I was too hot and angry to worry about confidentiality, if she wasn't. I told her that her son had been caught stealing a car, was in the detention center, and would be sent to the reform school within ten days. There was a pause, and then everyone was laughing. Oliver's mother was laughing. I didn't understand why, but later that evening I asked Oliver why his mother would laugh at such terrible news. "It's a game man, and I lost. It's no big deal."

As we talked I said I thought we had an understanding. I thought he was convinced that being a criminal was a losing proposition. He was kind and sincere when he gave me the facts of his life. All of that talk from him to me was jive, and he thought I knew it. "We live in two different worlds, man. I can't make it in yours and you can't make it in mine. You're the enemy. If I lie to you, or steal from you that's okay, cause it's a war. It's just like our country takes its people and goes and kills some other country's people to get what we want or to keep them from takin' what is ours. It's a war of gettin' what you can get, and you have to survive your way and I have to survive mine."

I thought I had been communicating, but as it turns out, I didn't know the language. I may have been slow then, but I was willing to learn from my mistakes. Over the next two weeks, I would see Oliver at least once a day. We talked about his world and my world, and now that I knew the ground rules, it was real communication. The facade was gone, and we began, for the first time, to understand each other.

A few days before Oliver was to go off to the reform school, I locked the keys in my car. I was bemoaning the fact to my office partner, but he started laughing. He told me that our profession had few advantages, but if you locked the keys in your car there were at least fifty kids just up the stairs who could retrieve them.

I told Oliver my problem, and asked if he could help. A broad smile grew on his face. I checked him out of detention, and we went to my car. Oliver reached down and removed a three-foot wire from the inside seam of his jeans. Within fifteen seconds my door was open and I had my keys. I didn't bother locking it again. Having witnessed that feat, any faith I may have had in the security of a locked car was destroyed.

When he was finished, Oliver started to put the wire back in his jeans, but I told him to give it to me. He looked at me with a disbelieving expression. "Hey, man, I just helped you out of a jam." I told him I appreciated his help, but he would have no need for the wire in reform school.

He smiled and said, "I guess you're catching on." I don't know what happened to Oliver, but I will be forever grateful for the seed of understanding that he imparted.

I thought I was communicating with Oliver, but I didn't know him or his world well enough to understand his language. I have seen this same process occur within family groups.

It is difficult to have a healthy family without clear, active communication, and every charlatan who claims to know something about human behavior tells the troubled parent to go home and communicate. The advice sounds good, and you walk out of his office reassured that you have just been given the answer, but when you try to put it into practice it fails. It fails because most families don't have much to talk about. Just telling people to communicate is like telling a golfer that his game would improve if he hit the ball better. Think about why you communicate with someone. What motivates you to say something to your child?

In many cases we talk to our children when we have an urgent need to provide instruction. "Don't drink beer and drive." "Don't have sex." "Don't speed." "Get your homework done." "Clean your room."

I hear parents say, "I talk to my kid all the time, but he won't listen." Our children will tune us out if 90 percent of what we say involves a do or don't. Establish a baseline of interaction so that your child doesn't become defensive the second you open your mouth.

What do I mean by a "baseline of interaction"? You could talk about your hobbies, fears, job, or friends. You could ask your child about her fondest dreams. Do you know her secret fears? Let her know where she sits in the family tree. It is important to talk about sex, drugs, AIDS, education, and her future, but you need to practice on less threatening subjects before you can tackle the big ones.

In the case of Karl R. and his son, Kip, the communication problem was exaggerated.

Young Kip was quickly becoming a well-known face in the courtroom. His father was a respected contractor in the community and a first-generation immigrant from West Germany. Kip started off as a shoplifter, but by his third appearance in court he had moved up to breaking and entering. It was obvious that the judge was getting restive and that the chances of institutional commitment were growing rapidly.

It was an important part of my responsibility as director of court services to monitor troublesome cases. I called in Kip's probation officer and asked what was going on. He was as confused as any of us. Just when he thought he was getting to the kid, he would be brought in on another charge. In every case Kip was involved with older boys. I told the officer to have the boy and his father in my office the next day. Kip's mother had died two years earlier. In preparation for the interview, I read through his case file. Kip was intellectually above average for a fourteen-year-old and was doing well in school. The usual miscreant behavior patterns were not there.

Kip was a handsome young man, and the family resemblance was striking. His father was of medium height, with big square shoulders, a square jaw, and a scowling brow that overshadowed brooding, dark eyes. Karl R. was definitely a formidable character. When I introduced myself, Kip said "Hi," and Karl grunted. Throughout the interview Karl grunted.

"Why do you think Kip is breaking into other people's homes?"

"Ugh."

"How do the two of you get along at home?"

"Ugh, Ugh."

I sent Kip out of the office and started over. When we were alone, I pointed out that the chances were very good that the judge would send Kip to the reform school if he was involved in another crime. I told him that he could sit there grunting or he could get involved and save his own son. He glared at me for a moment. I was getting anxious when I saw a big tear form in the corner of his eye. When he talked, the accent was so thick I could hardly understand him. He said that Kip was ashamed of his father and ashamed of their heritage. "Kip's real name is Wolfgang, but he is ashamed of his name and his father."

He kept repeating that his son was ashamed of him. I called Kip back in the room and told him what his father had told me. The child looked confused and embarrassed. I knew enough not to sit there and lecture two people who lived together but who otherwise were not acquainted.

The next day I paid a surprise visit to Karl on his job site, where he was the primary contractor for a large office building. He didn't see me standing off to the side. Karl was yelling at and laughing with his men. He could talk to his employees, but he didn't know how to talk to his son, even though the mutually caring relationship they had was obvious.

I had an idea, but it needed the judge's approval. I went back to the court, presented my plan to the judge, and received a special court order. I then picked Kip up at school and took him to his father. When Karl saw the two of us standing there, the blood drained from his face and he dropped the plans he was holding. I assured him that everything was all right, but for the rest of the school year young Kip would not go to school; instead, he would be working with his father. Karl said that was impossible; his son was going to be a college graduate, a professional man. I said that if he did not learn how to talk to his boy, his boy was going to be a criminal. I walked away.

That was May 1962 and I still get Christmas cards from both of them. Young Kip followed in his father's footsteps. Today they are still talking and are in business together.

Some experts claim that the problem is that parents do not listen to their children, and I agree. Other experts say that children do not listen to their parents, and I also agree with this. How, you may ask, is it possible for me to agree with both opinions? Easy. If neither is talking, how can the other listen?

As I have said, research has revealed that 80 percent of all communication in the average American family is nonverbal. Many children are almost completely inarticulate.

It is possible, in our complex modern world, for individual family members not to have mutual interests. Often we do not work together, play together, or get involved in community activities together. Many families no longer eat together. We each have our own little worlds, and when we try to share our special interest with other family members, they often turn a deaf ear. In a desperate attempt to have something to say, we talk about the weather or the news, but find it hard to say, "My feelings were hurt when I was shunned at the office today." It's hard to say, because we have learned from experience that no one seems to care. The average teenager would not consider telling her family that she just broke up with her boyfriend and hurt so bad that it was hard to breathe.

If you do not talk to your children, the family unit is not and cannot be a support system. Support is not money or a roof over our heads. Support is having a relationship with someone you can talk to, with someone you know is listening.

Couples with separate interests drift apart. This phrase had become a modern cliché. We accept the logic, and I never need to explain myself when I tell people that couples with separate interests drift apart. But when I say children and parents must have common interests or they too will drift apart, people are surprised. We can and do lose contact with our adolescent offspring if we do not maintain common interests. We can no longer blame the adolescent stage of life for all the distance that exists in our families. Some distance is necessary for normal growth, but most parents and children have all but lost contact. We must be sensitive to their pain and listen to their fears.

I made this point in a speech recently, and one of the mothers said she and her family listen all the time. They listen to radios and televisions. We get out of bed and turn on the radio or television because we hunger for the sound of the human voice.

Parents have to *work* at listening to what their children have to say. We teach our family-care parents to look at the child and block out other distractions while the child is talking. If it is not possible to listen properly, because the distractions are real and urgent, they tell them why they cannot give their undivided attention, and set up a time when they can communicate.

"My kid never talks to me."

"Why should I, you never listen."

"Never" seems to be one of the most commonly used words when we work with families in trouble.

How do families develop communication skills? You can start by learning to express some honest feelings and by making everyone in the family aware of this new project. Hold a family meeting and make a list of "feeling words" like *angry, happy, sad, anxious, hurt,* and *excited.* Have your family develop a list at least twenty-five words long, and when you ask family members how they feel, make them use a feeling word. "Fine" is not a feeling word, it is a cop-out.

I keep referring to the nonverbal communication that goes on in the average family. We depend on it too much, and it is not always a reliable way of communicating.

Father comes down to breakfast with dark rings under his eyes, a frown on his face, and heads for the car without saying good morning. Mother, Suzie, and John all think they know what is going on in Father's head. They assume they don't need to ask how he feels. Jane is certain the frown and dirty look is directly related to that dress she bought yesterday. Ralph said he liked it, but in reality he is angry because she spent the money. But, damn it, he bought a suit last week that cost $200, and you didn't see her complaining. If he comes home and says one thing, by God he's going to get it. Suzie is certain he is still angry at her for leaving the tricycle in the drive, and John is convinced that Father is having a fight with Mom, and he hates to come home from school when they are fighting. It's going to be a miserable day in school, knowing what he has to face when he gets home.

We are all so certain that we can read each other's minds, but we can't. If this family were willing to risk asking how Father felt, several issues *could* be resolved. What would have happened if this group had been prepared to probe for the man's real feelings?

"How do you feel this morning, Ralph?"

"I feel tired and anxious. I was up half the night worrying about my boss coming in to evaluate my work this morning. I have had to make some hard decisions lately, and I don't know if they are right or wrong." The father would not have caused the anxiety if he had said what was on his mind when he walked into the room.

In two sentences, Ralph explained to everyone why he was tired and looked angry. The paranoia disappears. The entire family could have had a bad day worrying about Father's anger. Jane would have been so worked up by the time he got home she would have picked a fight, and young John would have been certain that his reading of his Father's frown had been correct and would have had a terrible day, failing a spelling test and being even more upset when he got home.

In the meantime Ralph felt better for having expressed his worst fear. Ideally, Jane's attitude then shifts from defensive to supportive: "It doesn't make that much difference, Ralph, regardless of what the boss says or does, we will make it."

At this point you may be wondering whether you should confess anxieties like that in front of your children. John and Suzie feel frightened when they don't know what is going on, but after hearing their mother's calm, reassuring response, they feel relieved and reassured. Our children perceive our feelings without divining the source of those feelings. When they see happy or angry expressions they let their imaginations supply the reason.

It is difficult for us to express feelings. We feel naked and vulnerable when others know our inner fears or thoughts. The need to withhold one's feelings can be a kind of defense mechanism. What would have happened in this imaginary scenario if Ralph had said he was worried about being confronted by his boss, and Jane had said, "Oh my God, I've married a wimp. Can't you just stand up to your boss like a man?" The next time she asked Ralph to expose his feelings, the chances are he would not be very forthcoming.

When a family decides to communicate feelings, they assume a tremendous responsibility. Obviously, the parents cannot and should not expose all of their feelings and fears to their children. The adolescent will not share all feelings associated with his or her need for independence, or his or her feelings and fantasies about sex. All of us have private, personal thoughts that are ours alone.

For the family that decides to take the plunge, however, there will be thoughts shared that may sound funny to an adult, and you could go ahead and laugh, but don't expect the child to share again.

Sociologists have attributed the breakdown of the family to the beginning of the Industrial Revolution, when many small family businesses were dismantled. Before that the family worked together and depended on each other for their livelihood. One of the few strongholds in which that is still true today is the family farm. It has been my experience that children from healthy farm families seldom violate the law, commit suicide, or become emotionally disturbed. Farm families have shared experiences.

The rest of us must redevelop those skills and diligently maintain them.

There are seminars on communication. Businesses send their personnel managers and others to these seminars because they know that the business cannot operate efficiently if the individuals involved do not communicate with each other. The personnel manager is there to improve his skills so that he can solve business problems. The professional is not ashamed that his business has a problem that is in need of solution, and yet when it comes to family, we find it hard to admit to such a weakness.

There is an old movie called *I Remember Mama* that chronicles the life of an immigrant Swedish family living in San Francisco at the turn of the century. Mama was the lead character and the backbone of the family. Throughout the story, Papa would bring home the paycheck on Saturday night, and everyone would sit down with Mama to pay the bills. They would account for every penny, and when they were through, Mama would say, "Good the bills are paid, and we do not have to take any out of savings." Everyone would let out a sigh of relief. At one point the old maiden aunts came over to share some family gossip with Mama, and she insisted the children be allowed to listen; there were no secrets in her family. The movie was narrated by an actress who played the eldest daughter, and she told of a family that shared everything, which included that ultimate in taboo subjects, "money." They expressed their fears and joys. Mama set the tone and they were a healthy family. (The only secret that Mama kept was the fact that there never was a savings account.)

Healthy families *learn* how to communicate.

6

Good parents learn the dynamics of discipline.

When I talk with parents, their first question usually is: "How do I discipline my children when they resist everything I try? I provide a good structure, and my kid just tells me to get lost."

The word discipline is a red flag to parents and children. I was conducting an evaluation and consultation in one of our program sites and we started debating in loud, high-pitched voices the issue of discipline. The discussion focused on corporal punishment. No professional or surrogate parent in any of the programs I have been associated with is allowed to strike a child to control his behavior. Several of those present felt that this policy was like tying one hand behind their backs.

"When you have a sixteen-year-old boy standing up and spitting in your face as he tells you to go to hell, it's hard to not to give him a little swat to let him know who's in charge." I stopped the discussion and told them we were going to have a group exercise. I wanted them to take a five-minute break, think about how they were disciplined as children, and come back and share it with the others. When they came back they were very quiet, and by the time we were through, there were several who were sad or depressed by the remembrances. Some told of reasonable punishments and limits and how they were imposed, but others told of beatings, anger, and hurts that will never be forgotten. The discussion took on new depths as we realized the impact of disciplinary action on our own lives. If it is done impetuously and in anger, it can and does cause lasting damage to a parent-child relationship.

I would never advise that parents hide their anger from their children. Our children need to know how we feel, and be able to read from our expressions what we think about their behavior. They can monitor their actions if they can get a reading from us. But when you find it necessary to punish a child, thinking rationally and avoiding rash action will lead to the best results.

There is always a struggle between parents and children. The extent and intensity of that struggle depends upon the disposition of the child. With my own five children, I have had five totally different experiences, and as a result had to shape the discipline to the demands of each of them. There is no magic formula when it comes to discipline, but there are some ground rules that can be useful.

It took me many years to realize that the *struggle* is an important part of a child's growth. It is the emotional fertilizer that stimulates and enriches that growth.

When I started my first family-care home, I was obsessed with the notion that I would never be successful unless I could lessen, if not totally eliminate, the conflict that inevitably existed between the family-care parents and the children. I would watch, console, and agonize over these adults and kids as they went through their ritualistic dance of adjustment. Surrogate families deal with the same issues that come up in biological families, but these concerns are magnified by the damage already inflicted on the children. When a child first enters a group home, the home is a war zone where the *struggle* is a major factor.

Before I realized the actual value of this process, I tried to eliminate it. In one of our homes we hired a shift staff, individuals who would come in and work for eight hours a day and then go home while others took over. The conflicts in the house appeared to lessen immediately, and I was tempted to change the staffing patterns in the other homes posthaste, but held off to give the new staffing design a thorough test.

Within two months we noticed that the kids in the shift-staff house were not progressing. They were comfortable, but not growing. They were raising hell in the house and were being allowed to do so because the shift staff could leave the chaos and go home at the end of their eight-hour shift. There was no urgent need on the part of the supervisors to alter the inappropriate behavior. Since they didn't have to live with it, why should they? No one was pressing for conformity. No adult had made a commitment to the children. We actually began to see regression in the children. The *struggle* had been eliminated, and consequently growth had stopped.

When the surrogate parents move into our family-care homes, they are told that the first several months are going to be very difficult. If these people expect to maintain their sanity, and their house is to become a home, the kids will need to conform to some basic rules of conduct, and before that there will be a struggle. We support them and the children through the struggle, but if there is going to be any form of social order, the struggle will take place, and as long as children are growing and thinking, the conflict will continue, but at a controllable level.

All parents need to recognize the reality of this conflict and learn how to manage accordingly. Like stress, it will exist and the successful parents are those who learn to deal with it. You begin to see the handwriting on the wall when your one-year-old smiles as he reaches out to pinch your face, or when every other word out of your two-year-old's mouth is a resounding "No!"

The following are the personality traits and behaviors of people I have known who are good disciplinarians. No individual or couple has all the answers, but there are some basic guidelines that seem to work.

There are some people who have a self-assured quality about themselves that bespeaks confidence and strength. When we see them in action, it is easy to attribute their self-assuredness to some kind of mythical power, and we secretly wish that we too had this gift. When these confident people say they are going to accomplish a task, others believe it. When they ask others to do something, others do it. They are not loud or mean, and to add insult to injury, their dogs behave as well as their children.

If we try to evaluate their behavior or to identify the secret ingredient, we discover that these are the people who *follow through*. They are *consistent* and *do* what they say they are going to do. This is not a God-given gift but a learned behavior. If our children are to grow up with any sense of self-discipline, we had better learn this particular behavior.

Jon and Maria had been family-care parents in one of our homes in the Southwest for ten years. Physically and emotionally they are two of the most beautiful people I have ever known. Professionally, they are model parents and are often used as examples when we describe what good parenting is all about.

The children who come to our homes have been abused physically, emotionally, and sexually and/or have been abandoned by their parents. Two of the first children Jon and Maria received were brothers who had been beaten unmercifully by their father. The father told the judge that God and a television evangelist had said he should beat his boys. They behaved as though they had been raised by wolves. They didn't know how to eat at the table or sleep on beds. They had no social or educational skills and absolutely no trust of adults. When their intake material came across my desk, I called our director of that project and asked her what she thought our chances were of maintaining these young animals. "With anyone else, less than 10 percent, but with Jon and Maria, I think they will make it."

Two months later I visited the home. We try to get pictures of the children on the first day in residence, and we did in this case. The pictures were included in their intake material, but when I came into the house I did not recognize the boys. When I asked Jon where they were, he pointed to a child right in front of me who was sitting on the couch reading a book and to the other who was playing across the room with one of the girls on the floor. They did not look like the angry, hurt little boys in the pictures from the first day.

We went to the kitchen and I asked the burning question: How did you do it?

Jon said, "We let them know what we expect, and then we take it one day at a time."

Maria said, "And every day we said the same things, and did the same things, and pretty soon they learned."

It was too simple, so I asked for details. The example I remember best had to do with school adjustment. Within a month the boys were beginning to follow the routines at home and to feel secure, but were continuing to act out in school. Maria's solution to the problem was typical of their head-on style of parenting. She went to school with one of them and Jon went with the other. For the better part of a week they sat next to their children, and the boys began to function in school. As a follow-up, they sent them off each morning with one of the short performance forms, describing behavior expectations, with spaces for the teacher to check. Each evening Jon and Maria would sit with the boys and go over their daily report. They became star pupils, and one was awarded the student of the month award in his class.

If I had to describe their style of parenting in one word, it would be follow-through. And if it was two words it would be consistent follow-through. The children in Jon and Maria's house never doubt an instruction. When Jon and Maria say something should be done, it is done. These parents do not hit, yell, nag, or deprive their children of their own dignity. You could pick Jon and Maria's children out of a crowd. They smile more and possess a self-confidence that seems to radiate.

Children need to be cared for by someone who can lead. Good leaders establish fair structures and rules of conduct. Good leaders follow through.

Dr. Will Menninger, one of the founders of the Menninger Clinic, was the physician in charge of all military psychiatric cases during the Second World War. He came away from that experience convinced that the soldiers in platoons managed by officers who were strong leaders had fewer psychiatric casualties than those led by weak, insecure officers. Upon his return to the Menninger Clinic, Dr. Menninger applied that knowledge to industry. He and colleagues at the clinic developed a leadership seminar for the captains in industry. We need to create a leadership seminar for parents.

When we talk about discipline, we are addressing issues in leadership, not punishment. J. J. Heart was a leader, and her children flourished because of this. Even though young people resist the structures we impose, they feel secure when they are in the presence of adults who are in control.

But how do we, as parents, provide these appropriate disciplinary standards, and who can define what is and is not appropriate? Although the number one cause of family squabbles between spouses is money, a very close second is discipline. If you want to hear a good family argument, listen to a husband and wife debate the method and extent of punishment given to their errant child. However, the most effective disciplinarians are those who present a common front. When the child in trouble sees or feels the parents fighting over the various options related to the punishment, he has a natural tendency to try to split the parents. These attempts are often crude, and to an outsider they are so obvious they can be comical. But it is easy for the concerned parent to get caught in these seductive traps.

Carol comes home two hours late from a date. Mother and Father, worried sick, are sitting up in the living room when she walks in at two o'clock in the morning. Father immediately pronounces a one-month restriction. While this innocent child is standing with mouth open in disbelieving shock, she notices Mother's frown at this severe punishment. Immediately she turns to Mother, buries her head in her lap and begins to sob. Through these muffled sobs the parents hear a terrible story of automotive failure and incompetent garage mechanics. This whole tragic drama took place in a service station that had one phone, which was out of order. Carol's mother tells her to go to bed, and she will talk to Father. Father pulls himself out of his chair, goes to their room, and slams the door. Within minutes the husband and wife will be fighting about a problem that belongs to their daughter, but which the daughter has skillfully shifted to them.

Several issues emerge from this simple example. First, Carol was able to split her parents because her parents were vulnerable. We often use issues related to disciplining our children as an excuse to get at each other. When Mother stomps into the bedroom and tells Father that he jumped too fast and is a hardheaded, chauvinist pig, she is speaking as a wife, not as a mother. He may be a chauvinist pig, but that is another problem that should be addressed at another time. The primary agenda has shifted to her perception of what she doesn't like about her mate, instead of what needs to be done to discipline their daughter.

Second, Carol's father did act impulsively. Carol's parents had two hours of dead time, waiting for their daughter in the living room, to discuss the possible restrictions.

Third, father did not listen to his daughter's explanation before he pronounced his punishment. The excuse may have been logical or ridiculous, but she deserved the chance to tell her side of the story before her parents reacted to her behavior.

Fourth, it is obvious that Mother got sucked into her daughter's manipulative splitting. At the time, Carol was relieved to see that she could get Mom to team with her against the man who was going to clip her wings for one long month, but when the dust clears she will feel guilty, and more than a little insecure. If her parents are so weak as to fall for that kind of blatant manipulation, how sound are these people who are supposed to be guiding her life? She doesn't realize that Mother has her own agenda, and was waiting for an excuse to tell her husband that she did not like his arrogant attitude.

Fifth, what was Carol doing in the two hours between the end of the dance and the time she got home? She might have been at a gas station that did not have a phone, in a parked car experiencing her first contact with sex, or getting high on a drug that her boyfriend said was safe. These concerns are what kept her anxious parents sitting up in the living room waiting for her to come home. The concerns were never addressed. If the situation were handled differently, and one of these fears was in fact real, the parents would have the information necessary to deal with the problem. Yet again, they may have discovered that Carol was sitting out on a hill having a healthy conversation and sharing a few tender kisses.

It is easy for me to tell parents what they do wrong, but far more difficult to tell them how to do it right. There are as many opinions and attitudes toward discipline as there are thinking people in the world. Most of us claim we know very little, but in the heat of battle we become immediate experts.

My second child, Mark, is a horse trainer. He works with quarter horses and racing thoroughbreds. Over the past few years he has developed a reputation for being able to train the crazy ones. People from several states bring him horses that others have worked with but failed. I have watched with pride and awe as he gently brings out in these animals the best they have to offer. I recently asked him how he does it. Mark doesn't talk much, and simply said, "I let them know who's boss early, and then let up. If you go too far you take the spirit out of them, but if you're too easy you lose control and they are useless animals. Every one of them is different, and you have to do it the way it's right for them."

In a few simple words, Mark defined the key issues. No knowledgeable practitioner will ever write a book that will give you a step-by-step description of how to discipline *your* child, because people, like Mark's horses, are all different, and require various levels of control.

When we think about issues of discipline and try to define the primary reason for providing controls, we soon realize that most of us are motivated by our desire to *protect*, not punish. When our children are little we slap their hands when they try to put the keys in the light socket, or when they pull the lamp down on their head. When they get older we sit up half the night and put them on restriction because we are trying to protect them from drugs, bad companions, or AIDS. In the meantime the child is saying there is a great world out there, don't smother me. There is a fine line that must be walked if the discipline we provide is to produce a positive result. If you overprotect and overstructure, you will break their spirits. They will lose confidence in their ability to make decisions for themselves. Your subservient child will become someone else's yes-man. If, on the other hand, you turn them loose and assume they are going to make all of the right decisions on their own, you will be sorely disappointed. Children need structure and guidance.

We must first set the standard of behavior we expect our child to achieve, and then develop a strategy to reach that goal. This should be a conscious process, and you and your mate need to agree on some general parameters. Most of us assume everyone involved is already on the same wavelength, and that it would be a waste of energy, but there will come a time when you will be forced to sit down and talk about what behavior you expect from your children. This usually occurs when it becomes obvious that the cast of characters in your family have differing agendas.

I want my children to have manners, respect the rights and property of others, learn the skills necessary to have a base of knowledge that can be useful in any profession, and participate in shared work responsibilities. Just as they learn the value of structure in an orderly household, children learn most of their self-discipline from parents who are self-disciplined. They learn how to introduce their friends to each other. They learn and understand the value of work when they see their parents working. The rights and properties of others are respected according to the standard set by the adults in their life. Oliver, the car thief I discussed in Chapter 5, did learn from the adults in his environment; however, he learned the wrong things.

We assume too much, however, if we think our children will learn or live by a set of moral standards by simply observing. Under the direction of the best parents they will, on occasion, violate our rules and stomp all over our standards, but they will also be anticipating and wanting a response.

When I look up the word "discipline" in the dictionary, the first definition is a single word in capital letters: "Punish." The other definitions are full of strong words: "to bring under control—to impose order upon troops," also "to impose order upon."

How do we punish? What works?

When our children are small and behave inappropriately, we swat their pants to get their attention, and tell them "No." When they get to be school age, and the swats don't seem to have an impact, the parent is left with the choice of hitting harder or developing options. I will not insult the intelligence of the reader by giving a sermonette on the damaging effects of beating your child.

I do believe it is appropriate to physically restrain a child. If he is breaking up the furniture or kicking another person, he needs to be held or gently sat on until he can monitor his own behavior. When siblings are fighting, separate them before it comes to blows. The child does need to know that you are in control, and if you cannot demonstrate that control, he will be frightened and continue to act out until you have proved that you can stop him from hurting himself or others. If restraint is administered properly, and judiciously, the chances are that its use will not often be necessary. Our professional parents go through a training course in restraint. Eighty percent of the course focuses on developing the parents' ability to see trouble coming, so that physical contact will not be necessary. Most high-energy anger can be defused if authority is introduced early.

The punishment should fit the crime. If your daughter throws her sandwich on the floor, have her clean it up and mop the floor. If your son knocks a hole in the wall, have him fix the wall and pay the cost of the repair materials out of his allowance. When you go with him to buy the repair materials, and supervise the work, you may end up getting to know each other better. These are the moments when you can calmly ask why he was so angry that he felt the need to put his fist through the wall. If Carol comes home late and does not have a valid reason, restrict her next date to a Coke date in the kitchen. If Carol demonstrates that she cannot handle being out on her own, you will help by being there to remind her of the time.

Be calm, and think before you act.

It was a cold winter day twenty years ago when I walked into the middle of an upset in one of our houses. I can't remember all of the specifics of the incident, but I will never forget the manner in which it was handled. Allie, the family-care mother, was in the house alone. She was five feet tall, and it would be stretching it to think that she weighed more than one hundred pounds. Standing over her, yelling in her face, was Sid the barbarian. Sidney had wild blond hair and bright blue eyes, and had come to our program with a temper that was notorious. He was six four and two hundred forty-five pounds, and his massive shoulders and protruding jaw could intimidate most grown men. Allie told Sid that he could not go out that evening, because he had not done his homework or completed his chores. He was yelling obscenities and pointing his finger. Allie stood there looking him in the eye, and talking in a calm, slow, moderate tone. He would yell he was going anyway, and she would say, "No, Sid, you need to stay home and get your homework done."

This kind of exchange continued for twenty minutes while I watched. Her quiet tone was not mocking, and the expression on her face was as calming and reassuring as the soothing voice. It was a piece of art. Sid calmed down and went to his room to study. Until it was over, neither one of them knew I was there. I have since noticed that the good family-care parents seldom yell, and their instructions do not include a challenge, nor are they laced with hostility.

Sidney graduated from high school and later joined the Army. I was in the house the day he came home on his first leave. By then he was a handsome, well-groomed young man. We were all proud of him, and I saw the tears glaze his eyes when Allie walked in the kitchen. When he hugged her, her feet were two feet off the ground.

You don't have to be angry to punish. Keep calm, speak quietly, and do not mock, nag, or set up a challenge like: "If you don't get your homework done I'm going to . . ." Most young people will not be able to resist finding out whether you mean it. They love a dare. If you have a rule, simply state it, and *when* they violate the rule, then determine the punishment.

Obviously, every parent is working toward the ultimate goal of imbuing within his or her children a sense of self-discipline. It will happen if you have the courage to follow through and maintain consistent expectations.

Once the expectations are understood, you can say to your children, "You can fly to the moon, if you can handle it," and they will understand the limitations of such freedoms.

7

*Parents who focus
on negative behavior and ignore
the positive create within their child
a poor self-image.*

Delinquent children come in all sizes, shapes, colors, and intellectual capacities, but there is one personality trait common to most kids who get in trouble: a very poor self-image. Whether we call it poor ego strength or lack of self-confidence, the malady is too common to ignore when we try to understand why some children rebel and strike out in anger at the rest of society.

How do people develop this poor self-image? Are they born with it? Is it the result of a chemical imbalance? No! and No! We decide who we are and what we are worth by evaluating the reactions of those we care about. Other people are the mirrors to our understanding of self. If we look into the face of the person we are interacting with and see disgust, we assume we are disgusting. If we look and see anger, we assume we are bad. If we look and see acceptance and love, we assume we are good.

In spite of the best intentions, it is natural for all of us to react spontaneously to negative behavior. When a child misbehaves it is disruptive. When you are trying to relax and read the evening paper and your kid is bouncing his ball off the bedroom wall or making the roof vibrate with the noise from his new stereo, you react. If, on the other hand, you are reading the paper and your child is sitting at the kitchen table doing his homework, there is no need to react. Quiet does not beg a response.

For those parents who have never really considered the issue, the problem can be solved by getting into the habit of verbalizing our appreciation of our children's good behavior, as well as correcting their poor behavior. They need to know what we like if they are to comply with our expectations. Children are not mind readers. Telling them what we do not like does not make clear what we do like. At the same time, telling parents to develop a new behavior pattern and to learn to accentuate the positive is overly simplistic, and in many cases nonproductive. This was brought home to me several years ago by an unlikely source.

Mary Sue P. was a member of a governor's juvenile justice task force. I was a consultant with the group and had worked with them for the better part of a year when she asked for a few minutes of my time. Her fourteen-year-old son had been arrested two days earlier for assault and battery. It was his third arrest, and she was at the end of her rope. Mary Sue confessed that she had accepted the assignment to the task force in hopes of learning something that would help her with her own son. John had been a problem for ten years, and she and her husband had run out of resources. The boy had seen three psychiatrists and two social workers and had been under the supervision of four different probation officers. He had been evaluated and reevaluated so many times that he knew the answers before the questions were asked. It is important to note that the focus of each of these interventions was on the boy John. John was the problem, so it seemed logical to look at John.

Mary Sue asked if I would come to dinner and casually observe her son. As far as he would be concerned, I would only be a dinner guest. I declined, saying I would not learn anything that the other, more-qualified professionals did not already know, and I would not partake in the deception. I asked Mary Sue how she would feel if her husband brought someone in to observe her under the guise of being a dinner guest. She understood completely and was embarrassed for being so callous.

We talked for three hours. By the end of the third hour, I was confused but determined. I was assuming that she was being honest. I knew this lady, and she was too desperate and too down to lie. Mary Sue P. was well educated, and because of her professional background, she knew more about child development than I would ever know. By this time I was curious and could not simply walk away, professing ignorance. I asked her to go home and bring John to the meeting room in the hotel I was staying in.

John was about what I had expected—angry, but more bored than hostile. He ignored most of my questions and grunted at others, but the shocker was not John, it was Mary Sue. In her son's presence she was a different woman than I had known for the past year. I told John to wait for us in the hotel lobby. I told his mother that it was obvious that she was angry with her son and that she had better figure out why before they spent any more money on evaluations for John. Again, she outlined John's miscreant behavior and asked what parent would not be infuriated.

I pointed out that the rejection I saw encompassed far more than her anger at the immediate situation. Mary Sue stomped out of the room, and I boarded the plane the next day, knowing I had once again overstepped my boundaries and professional expertise.

Six months later Mary Sue and her husband Bob walked into my office. Bob was attending a meeting in a nearby town and she had come along, knowing it was close to where I lived. She had left my hotel room six months earlier and had gone home and told Bob what a jerk I was. Bob agreed but asked what had prompted the discovery. When she told him what I had said, he reminded her that the three psychiatrists, two social workers, and three of the four probation officers had implied the same thing. Perhaps it was time to face that the problem might not be John.

Mary Sue and Bob went into individual therapy, and they and their son were working with a family therapist. One thing they discovered was that Mary Sue P. resented her son. His presence disrupted her career. Before he was born she was a nationally recognized expert on early childhood development. She traveled extensively and received most of her personal gratification from being recognized as an expert. It did not matter that the expertise should have given her the insight to see her own problem.

She was in her early thirties when she and Bob decided to have a baby. As a direct result of her professional conviction, she made the decision to stay home and sacrifice her career. She thought she knew the value of full-time mothering. But she neglected her own needs, as well as the warning signals that surfaced when negative feelings toward her son began to emerge. On the other hand, young John knew immediately that his mother was not happy with him, and when he was old enough he began to act out his understanding of badness. Children usually behave the way their parents expect them to behave.

As I said earlier, it is possible to emphasize the negative and to forget to mention the positive out of ignorance. But, as in the case of Mary Sue and her son, John, the negative output, both verbal and emotional, can be based on unconscious resentment. She loved her son, but she also resented him. She cared for her son, but his very presence reminded her of her loss. Unconsciously, she blamed him for imprisoning her in a restricted world. It was her guilt, not his presence, that had led to the banishment from her profession, but John felt the resentment without knowing the reason for it.

This case occurred twelve years ago. Today, we see this type of situation with a regularity that is as frightening as it is monotonous. We are beginning to see a large number of children growing up in households where one or both of the parents resent their child's presence.

More young, upper-middle-class professionals are having babies today. These same men and women often create for themselves fairly structured lives before the baby's arrival. Their world revolves around their careers and self-fulfillment. All at once they can no longer go play when they want, and if both are still working, the wife can resent the energy required to be a mother. Often, her career suffers, and her husband sails on as if nothing had happened.

At a time when parenting demands and requires more time and thought, these parents have less time and energy to give. The child can be perceived as an unwelcome invader of their world. When we resent our child's very existence, we accentuate the negative. Everything that child does is negative. It is a no-win situation for parent and child.

All of this sounds rather alarming, but the good news is that most of us can be helped, because most of our negative attitudes have nothing whatsoever to do with our children. We accentuate the negative because we have been stomped on so many times that we feel hurt and rejected. When we get in that state of mind, we don't dismiss our feelings as paranoia, we know the world really does hate us. Our career isn't going as planned, but we decide to stick it out for the retirement benefits. Our marriage is dull, and the local football team hasn't had a winner in twelve years, but we still go to the games because we are starting to enjoy booing the bums. The only person we can identify with is Rodney Dangerfield, but his jokes are too real to be funny. We "just don't get no respect." When we are trapped in this kind of negative thinking, we react to our children in the same way, and they go into the world handicapped by a poor sense of self.

The following scenario is one that school counselors witness at least once a week.

CHILD: "I don't know why I'm that way, I'm just not any good. I can't do anything right."

COUNSELOR: "Why do you think you are bad?"

CHILD: "I don't know, I just am. Ask my dad, he knows I can't do anything right."

The mother and father sit there with an expression of dumb disbelief. They cannot believe their kid is sitting there telling this stranger that he feels useless, when deep in their negative hearts, they feel he is a damn fine child. Sure, they complain about his behavior all the time, but how else is he going to learn to do it right.

PARENT: "How can you say you are bad? Where do you get these ideas?"

CHILD: "Oh come on, Dad, you tell me what a useless piece of shit I am all the time. I don't do anything right, my room's a mess, I have pimples that would go away if I would clean my face. I know it's not your fault, that's just the way I am. I want to be the son you want, and for a while I tried, but I just can't get there."

I have seen these conversations turn into therapeutic experiences for parent and child if each has the presence of mind to listen to the other. The parents often see how their negative responses to most of what their child does affect his self-concept and behavior. But even if the light does go on and the parents are, for the first time, aware of the impact of their negative reactions, how do they change an established pattern of behavior? By this time in their life, the sour disposition and the negative attitude may have become a very real part of their personality. There are those who find real satisfaction in their bad attitude, and swell up with pride when they hear themselves being referred to as a "hard case." Anything less than that is to be labeled a wimp.

But it is possible to change, and I have seen what can happen when people learn to develop a positive attitude. I have seen negative souls climb out of their depressive existence.

During the time I worked with Dr. Karl Menninger, I met a gentleman by the name of W. Clement Stone. He had created an insurance empire, and was considered one of the wealthiest men in America. W. Clement Stone's presence in national politics had launched presidents, and his philanthropic endeavors for charities and the arts had become legendary. He had asked Dr. Menninger to aid in the development of an innovative mental health center on South Michigan Avenue in Chicago. Dr. Menninger, in turn, had asked me to assist in the creation of the youth programs. I had heard of Mr. Stone long before I met him, and most of those who knew him or his reputation sang his praises. The only dissenters were a few pseudo-sophisticates who would snicker at what they considered his one idiosyncratic behavior. W. Clement Stone was an avid believer in PMA, positive mental attitude. This was not a passing fancy. PMA was a way of life for this man, and those who worked for him were almost as fanatical in this philosophy of life as Mr. Stone.

I once accompanied Dr. Menninger to one of Mr. Stone's corporate board meetings. Karl gave no warning of what was in store as we entered the elaborate board-room filled with handsome, manicured men in pinstriped suits. Each one greeted us cordially as they stood to be introduced. We sat to one side, away from the corporate officers surrounding the huge table, and were talking quietly to each other when Mr. Stone walked in.

He had a gentle smile on his face, and he opened his mouth and said, "Good morning, how do you feel this morning?" The pinstripes straightened up and in a half shout said, "Great! Great! We feel great!" I sat there too dumbfounded to react. Throughout the meeting these men would shout their approval after a positive report from one of their colleagues. They were reinforcing each other in a way I had never seen people do, and it worked. Before the meeting was over, I was starting to feel the effects of this vociferous interaction. Finally one gentleman stood to give a negative report on the sales in his area. When he was through, Mr. Stone asked what he had learned from the experience. The vice president was prepared and gave a thorough account of what he had learned, and when he was through, Mr. Stone and the group applauded their colleague.

All the time I worked with Mr. Stone, I never knew a situation that he considered negative. He would take a disaster and turn it into a triumph. His daughter, Donna, lived by her father's golden rule, and when she was a young woman she announced to the world that she was going to create the National Council on Child Abuse. Critics said she had neither the training nor the skill to tackle such an ambitious endeavor. Today, the council is one of the most effective voices for children in this country.

Many of the people who had come into contact with W. Clement Stone and other positive thinkers, like Norman Vincent Peale, have become converts. People who had given up on life and felt they were failures became successful in business, but more important, they learned to like themselves.

Yes, I am proposing that good parenting requires a positive attitude. There are several books that can be of value, and if you accentuate the negative and feel the world is going to hell in a handbasket, get them and read them. It may sound like a simple idea, but I have seen it work too many times to discount its merits.

There is a small village in Scotland that has a charming tradition. When anyone in the village dies, the other residents gather at the grave and say something positive about the deceased before the casket is lowered. It went without a hitch for generations, but a problem arose, and the community was not sure the tradition could continue uninterrupted. The problem, in this case, was a mean old hermit who lived at the top of the hill. He was so mean and so hateful that no one could think of a positive thing to say. He finally died. They stood over the casket for three hours in total silence. Finally someone said, "Well, I guess he could have been worse," and the relieved community lowered the body.

There are times when it is difficult to think of something positive to say about your child, especially during the teen years. He has a bizarre haircut, listens to loud noises he refers to as music, talks back, insists on living in a dirty room, and does what he can to mess up the rest of the house. Many go further by getting involved in drugs, stealing the clothes they want, or allowing their bodies to be abused in indiscriminate sex. Parents everywhere end up wondering if they could even say, "He could have been worse." And then I come along and out of one side of my mouth tell you it is important to provide structure and out of the other say you must be positive with your child. Is it possible to do both?

People who internalize a positive outlook go through their daily routine with an invisible protective shield. Their spouse, their work associates, and their children may, through aggressive behavior, attempt to penetrate that shield, but the undaunted optimist will win out. They have an inner strength that continues to radiate through good times and bad. The best part of this phenomenon is that the optimistic attitude is catching. The optimist will, in the end, influence the feelings and attitudes of those around him.

Every day J. J. Heart, the singing family-care parent, would warble in an off-key voice instructions that were not always obeyed. She, like many good parents, had two basic rules: First, keep it consistent, and second, keep it pleasant. You don't have to be angry to maintain discipline. She would kindly tell the kids to clean their room, and when they didn't, she would just as kindly tell them their allowance was $2 short because they hadn't done it. J. J. Heart *believed* that every child who came to her home was capable of being a caring, useful person. She and her husband have had children spit in their faces and been cursed and hit by children who had no faith in themselves. But J.J. would come back with a smile. She may have been sitting on their bodies at the time, but she was smiling. In time her positive mental attitude would overcome their negative feelings about themselves, and they would leave her home feeling good about themselves.

You can tell children that they have a bad attitude without telling them they are bad. You can say their behavior is inappropriate without conveying the notion that they are dirty and worthless. When four-year-old Jeff pushes his two-year-old sister down and throws her doll in the mud, you could say, "Jeff, you are a mean, hateful bully, and I am ashamed of you." Jeff will then assume he is a mean, hateful bully, and accept his parents' judgment. After all, his parents are the boss. If, a few minutes later, someone were to ask Jeff what he was, he would say he was a mean, hateful bully.

Do not assume that young Jeff considers this new identity as all bad. His sister was getting all the attention, and the adults were saying what a cute thing she was. When he pushed her down, and threw the doll in the mud, it felt good. Being a mean, hateful bully feels good. Your angry words were meant to help Jeff see the error of his ways and change his behavior, when in fact you may have reinforced the behavior. Once he was labeled, there was nothing left to talk about. You passed judgment, and he accepted the judgment.

What would have happened if you had said, "Jeff, why did you do that? You're a nice boy, and you love your sister. That kind of angry behavior doesn't help anyone. If you're upset, tell me and we can talk about it, but a good boy like you doesn't need that kind of angry behavior." It is the behavior that's bad, not Jeff. You can be just as stern as you talk about the behavior as you were when you talked about the boy. In this instance you have left the door open for Jeff to talk about his anger, and you have reinforced the notion that he is a good boy.

I have seen the angry, defensive, timid children that come from homes where negative parenting dominated. And I have seen these same children grow and blossom into confident people when exposed to positive parenting.

8

Good parents like themselves and know how to laugh.

Children who grow up in homes where one or both parents are habitually glum, angry, or depressed blame themselves for their parents' miserable personality. Homes like these are hot-house incubators where tomorrow's neurotics are developed. Parents can maintain structure, follow through on discipline, and cultivate all the parenting skills outlined in this book, but if they are unhappy or depressed while they do it, their children will neither appreciate nor benefit from any of it.

Over the past twenty years I have been involved in hiring at least three hundred sets of surrogate parents for the various programs we have established throughout the country. I continue to interview many applicants myself because our ability to identify the qualities that make a "good parent" is crucial to our success. Before a couple is considered for employment, they must have two qualities that we consider to be essential: a true affection for themselves and a sense of humor. Somehow the two go together, and we have never found one without the other.

We have hundreds of applicants who hang their heads as they state their dedication to the cause of better child care. With glum faces, they profess their willingness to attend to the needs of our lost and lonely waifs, in spite of the pain involved in providing that care. These are the people who think of parenting as a chore, a dreaded task that requires a superhuman commitment. Many of these unhappy believers feel that they have the will to withstand the rigors of parenting these troubled creatures because of their faith in some kind of angry god. Apparently, they feel that if they expose themselves to enough pain in this world they will have a better place in the next. In the beginning of the program, I hired a few of the living saints and found that *they* lasted, but the children under their care did not. No one wants to live with a grouch.

The truth is that people who do not know how or have lost the ability to laugh at themselves and their own condition lose sight of what is important. Parents cannot demonstrate love for their children if they do not love themselves. Martyrs make miserable parents. Throughout my career I have seen some startling examples of this truth, but none more obvious than a particular young man whose circumstances kept me confused for several weeks.

Seventeen-year-old Edward P.'s rap sheet looked like an applications form for the "Who's Who" of young criminals. It ranged from armed robbery to shoplifting, but there was no consistent pattern. Edward seemed to go for any crime as long as someone else had the idea and there was at least a 90-percent chance of getting caught. The juvenile court had committed him to the reform school where I was superintendent, and after evaluating his case, I concluded that we were dealing with one of those people who could get high scores on IQ tests but who was otherwise dumb as a stump. His father, Roger, was a university professor, and his mother, Jane, was a homemaker.

In was the early 1960s, and in those days it was a rarity to see upper-middle-class children actually sent to reform school, regardless of the number of crimes they had committed. In this case, the boy had outlasted the patience of the court. He had been released from detention and placed on probation so many times that the judge was becoming embarrassed.

When the young deputy brought Edward in to the institution, they were chatting like old friends and parted laughing. I was anticipating a traumatized kid quaking at the notion of being shipped off to our state's most notorious penal facility, but to look at his face you would have thought he had just been dropped off for his freshman year in college. He was amiable, curious about the accommodations, and obviously bright. I couldn't figure out what made this young man tick, but I thought I had the answer when I concluded that he must be one of those sociopathic personalities. (We don't call them that anymore, but it was big in the sixties.) If that were the case, he would have no conscience and no sense of remorse, and would be capable of conning anyone who wasn't especially alert. With this snap diagnosis as an excuse, I immediately warned the staff to be on their toes: "Watch this kid, he'll act nice and do just about anything to get his way."

I was at least half right: Edward was nice and seemed to be having a good time, but he wasn't manipulating anyone. What the hell did we have? To see his smiling face every morning at breakfast was disconcerting.

Finally, in complete bewilderment, I called him into my office and asked him why he was so damn happy. Edward was open and articulate. He was happy because he was not at home with a mother who was an absolute shrew. His mother, Jane, was a bitter, mean, and angry person. Because of her, his oldest sister had killed herself two years earlier, and another sister, who was a year younger than Edward, was in a private psychiatric hospital. Each child had found a unique escape. It did not take long to find out that everything young Edward said was true. The reform school was a vacation spot compared to the miserable home in which he had grown up.

When I talked to Edward's father he said he was sorry he had allowed his children to be hurt by this woman, but he took his marriage vows seriously and did not know what to do. Three children were abused because a father took his marriage vows seriously and an angry, bitter woman refused to seek help. I told the father to notify his relatives that his son was in a reform school, and that I would release Edward in their custody if they agreed to assume the responsibility for his care. Within forty-eight hours we had responses from two uncles and the paternal grandmother. Edward chose to live with an uncle on a desolate ranch in the northern part of the state. He is now the owner of the ranch and a county commissioner.

Children do not like to live with unhappy people. I am not talking about parents who respond negatively to their children's behavior, as in Chapter 7. I am talking about parents whose primary emotion is anger or depression.

One of our directors called at ten-thirty one night and apologized for interrupting my evening, but knew she could not sleep if she didn't talk about a problem that was nagging her. She was concerned about a set of family-care parents who had been with her program for over a year, but confessed that when she tried to put her fears into words it sounded stupid. She had called to complain about them, but all she did was tell me all the things they were doing right. They set a good structure, followed through on discipline, and observed all the rules listed in the manual of operations. Yet all of her instincts told her to get them out of the house and away from the children. She was in the office when she called, so I asked her to go to her personnel files and read what I wrote in the initial interview notes. I knew the couple in question; I had been present when they were hired. There was a short pause, and then I heard her laughing. My notes, which I remembered, consisted of a five-word sentence.

"These people are too grumpy."

After she stopped laughing she acknowledged that this was true, but she felt it was not a good enough reason to fire them. I then told her to use a guideline that I had used throughout my career: If something happened to me and my wife, and no other living relative were there to care for my children, would I feel good about my children going to live in this couple's home? She fired them the next day.

If your car is broken, you fix it. If your roof leaks, you patch it. But when it comes to ourselves, all too often we ignore or bury our real concerns. We accept depression as a way of life. There is a popular bumper sticker that says: "Life's a Bitch—and Then You Die." There are too many people who believe it. It's not funny, and I don't think it was meant to be funny. Many people *are* unhappy, but not so much with the world as with themselves. They may use the political climate or crime on the streets as an excuse for their sour faces, but in fact they are miserable from the inside out.

If you were to ask the average parent what he wanted for his child, the universal response would be "To be happy." A good parent wants his offspring to go through life doing what he wants and being happy. But don't forget, your parents wanted the same for you. You are someone's child.

When you ask children what they want for their parents, the response is "To be happy." Your children will not be content if you are miserable.

Quite frankly, I am not sure what "happy" is, but I do know that people do not find inner peace or contentment until they like themselves. How do we acquire this appreciation and respect for ourselves? If you believe the ads on radio or television, you will find self-respect and joy in life if you take the right pill, wear the right bra, or drink the right beer. Advertising agencies create illusions designed to persuade the public that one particular product will be the quick and easy way to happiness. But if we take the time to look beyond these shallow fantasies, we discover that one of the primary reasons for our discontent is the loss of control of our own environment. We feel like victims in just about every aspect of our life. We don't like the job or our boss, but swallow our pride for the paycheck that pays the bills. We don't like the city we live in, but that is where the job is. We don't like our bodies, but we don't have the time or the energy left to exercise them. You may want to make your own list of personal management problems and the chronic excuses that keep you from taking command of your own life.

One of my favorite movies in the past several years is *Crocodile Dundee*. When I saw this picture, I laughed and cheered and envied this amazing character. Crocodile Dundee was a man who mastered his own environment. He was no one's victim. It didn't matter if he was in the Outback in Australia wrestling with crocodiles or on the streets of New York City confronting muggers: He was in command. His self-confidence and quiet, simple sense of dignity seemed to cut through all of the societal clutter. He would dominate any and all circumstances, because he had self-confidence, and the skills to back up this sense of self. We admired him because he was in control of his own destiny. No circumstance seemed to change who or what he was.

There are no Crocodile Dundees, but there are some people who are satisfied with who they are and have a real appreciation for what they have become. If we take a look at these individuals, we discover that as a group they have some common qualities.

These confident personalities have a secure sense of emotional self. They are not burdened with crippling neuroses. In some cases this emotional security is natural; they were raised by parents who were secure, happy people and simply passed it on to their children. With others it took some introspection or professional help to gain control of their emotional self.

But few of us emerge from childhood totally free of emotional hang-ups. Many of the guilt feelings and unnatural fears that we carry with us can be debilitating. We can be morose and unhappy because at an early age our parents or our religion said that we should be that way. This philosophy of life implies that if you are happy you are obviously doing something wrong. Or if you were told over and over that you were a bad person, you may believe deep down inside that you are a bad person.

A full list of the offenses that can lead to our hang-ups and eventual discontent would require several volumes but if you are going to respect yourself, you need to put your emotional house in order and dump this excess baggage. I have seen too many parents go through life bent and bruised from guilt and fear that they, in turn, pass on to their offspring. If you are going to learn to like yourself, you need to look at your physical well-being. We can be miserable when we don't take care of our bodies. We can get downhearted when we smoke too many cigarettes, or drink too many drinks, both of which are scientifically guaranteed to depress. We can turn sour when our blood finds it hard to flow around all the junk food residue to the multiple fat layers.

Several years ago, Paul Harvey, the radio commentator, told of a middle-aged gentleman who became depressed and decided to kill himself. But he was faced with a dilemma. He was a devoted family man and didn't want his loved ones to be hurt by a suicide, and he wanted the life insurance people to think he had died of natural causes. One day he heard a doctor tell people not to start a heavy jogging routine if they had not been exercising since the exertion might kill them. Early the next morning he rolled out of bed, put on his old tennis shoes, and hit the streets. He had gone half a block when he fell to the curb exhausted. The following morning he went two blocks, and by the third morning he was up to half a mile (about ten blocks). By this time he was starting to feel good, decided against suicide, and confessed his original plot to his wife. The next morning he went out to jog, was hit by a truck, and died.

I know it's a bad story, and the fact that I have remembered it all these years shows what a morbid sense of humor I have. But I cannot tell you how many friends I have had who were middle-aged, depressed, decided to exercise, and felt great as a result. It is amazing how much better one feels when the blood does start flowing. We live in a exercise-crazed society, and it is tempting to say it's a fad for the young and eager, but in fact it is here to stay for all ages. There are too many people out there on the streets walking, bicycling, or jogging to discount it as a passing fancy. If you talk to these active individuals, you will hear from smiling faces that they are feeling good about themselves.

When I talk about exercising, I am referring to the moderate version. I don't run ten miles, five times a week. I walk three miles, four times a week. People who set unrealistic goals will either burn out or become compulsive exercisers, which can be dangerous and unhealthy. Go out and buy one of those new fifteen-speed mountain bikes that look like the old fat-tire versions that we used to spend all day riding when we were kids. It is fun, and you may be surprised at how much better you feel. Don't do it to lose fifty pounds and look like a movie star. Do it because the whole physical self will function better, and when the body feels good, the mind has a chance to breathe and get some fresh blood. You feel good from the inside out.

It is important for people to enjoy their work. I do not mean to imply that those of us who get some gratification from our profession are in a constant state of euphoria or that there aren't pitfalls in all trades, but if you get out of bed every morning dreading your job, you cannot maintain a healthy outlook on life. It will wear you down. You may be using the excuse that you are doing it for the family, but the family, if given a choice, would probably prefer a smaller paycheck and greater satisfaction for the parent.

An old friend, John S., was an accountant. He hated counting, money, enclosed offices, and meetings. We were both in our mid twenties, and John had just become a CPA. To anyone who knew John and his wife, Terry, they would have seemed the perfect couple with perfect kids. Late one evening he came to my house to tell me he and Terry were getting a divorce. They were incompatible, and had begun to drift apart. He took three minutes to tell me about his marital problems, and forty minutes to express how very much he hated his work. When I asked what he wanted to do, he laughed. All his life he had dreamed of being a forest ranger, but had never told anyone, including Terry. I told him to go home and tell his wife what he wanted to do, and to think about the real problem.

Apparently, they spent the night talking, and within a week he had reenrolled in college. They stayed together, and Terry encouraged his change of career in midstream. He will never make as much money, but he is happy. Terry is now an accountant, and she loves it. This sounds like a fairy tale, and many who read it will scoff at the notion that people have that kind of control of their destiny. Terry and John made sacrifices to get what they thought was important. The question is whether you are willing to give up short-term security for future satisfaction.

People who plop down in a chair and withdraw into television or booze to forget the day make lousy parents and miserable spouses.

Individuals who have a healthy respect for themselves know how to interrelate with other people. When we interview prospective family-care parents, we ask them why they want the job. If they say they enjoy being with kids and other assorted types of people, we know we have a real prospect. Good parents have an active social and recreational life. It doesn't matter whether it's fishing, bridge, investment clubs, stamp collecting, golf, or rugby; the important thing is their enthusiastic interaction. The capacity to have fun is, like positive thinking, contagious.

We also ask the prospective parents what they do on a Saturday night. If they tell us about the relatives or friends who come over for bridge or to barbecue a steak, we know they have a healthy support system. People who respect themselves maintain relationships with friends and relatives. In our mobile society, it is difficult to maintain close friendships, but those who work at it reap the rewards. Most of us will develop a relationship if someone approaches us, but are reluctant to take the first step. We are living by the old high school popularity theory. "If

they really like me they will call." In the meantime everyone is waiting, and no one is calling. Go to a house where
a group of adults are sitting around the kitchen table having a lively conversation, and I will show you kids in other
parts of the house and yard having a good time.

Good parents have, or learn to have, a healthy respect
for themselves.

9

Successful kids come from nurturing homes.

The ability to nurture is not an option: It is essential if you want to raise healthy children. Unlike most of the other parenting skills described in this book, nurturance is a part of the basic equipment. I believe you are born with the instinctive ability to nurture, even though negative life experiences can and do blunt these skills.

Nurturance is the emotional life-giving blood that stimulates sound, well-conditioned mental and physical growth. It is the spiritual quality in parenting, the undefinable element that separates the good from the bad and the adequate from the inadequate. Parents can excel in all of the other skills, but if they cannot nurture, their children will not be physically or emotionally healthy.

What is this magic quality called nurturance? It is the force that motivates you to prepare and serve the best food possible, even though your child may consistently reject the product and the effort. Nurturing parents have the uncontrollable urge to touch and kiss their children's dirty faces. It is the instinct to comfort when the children are sick, to hold and soothe them when they are frightened. Those who nurture best do a lot of touching and kissing, and their children feign embarrassed postures, but these same children are the secure ones, the leaders, the learners, the kids with smiles on their faces. Those who nurture know when their child is sick before the onset of fever or that the child hurts inside by the expression on her face or by the way she walks. And when they sense a problem, they respond immediately rather than turning away, hoping it will disappear.

I began to put a high value on nurturance when I was the director of juvenile court services. As the director, I was also responsible for the maintenance of the detention home. The court offices were housed in the basement of the ancient county courthouse. We had three tiny rooms stuck deep in the damp basement that housed six probation officers. The detention home was a half a block away. To get there, we walked through the furnace room and out the back door. It was a giant old brick house with small windows. Most of the yard was a gravel drive where the police and sheriff's officers would slide to a dusty stop to deposit their miniature prisoners. This was the facility where we held the delinquents who were too tough to allow back on the streets, and also the place where social workers brought neglected children after they were abandoned or beaten. The combination of this clientele was absolutely combustible, and the notion of keeping frightened, neglected children in the same building with angry, hostile delinquents was preposterous.

When I took the position, I was twenty-four years old, but the grand and all-inclusive knowledge that I had taken into the job in Kansas City had already been tempered by the realities of the kids and the system. By the time I took this responsibility, I had downgraded my self-assessment and knew that being the director of court services was a major task. I was not all that sure I was up to it.

We had just finished the three-minute tour of the small, ratty office space, when the judge said I was also responsible for the supervision of the detention home. There I was, trying to decide if I was up to this major task when my new boss, in a few simple words, doubled my responsibilities. It was a dark, rainy day. With our heads under our suit coats, we ran the forty yards across the muddy courthouse parking lot to the detention home. When I stopped at the back door, which was the only door that anyone used, I looked up at the old three-story house and shuddered. If I took omens seriously, I would have thanked the judge for the tour and walked away. But I needed the work, and by this time my curiosity was piqued.

We walked in and he introduced me to a pleasant lady standing over the stove cooking grilled cheese sandwiches. The sandwiches looked great and I silently thanked God that we at least had a good cook. On the first floor there was a kitchen, dining room, living room, office, and apartment for the live-in director. On the second floor there were two large dorms for boys and girls on the front side of the house, two bathrooms next to the dorms, and four gray steel cells, with doors made of bars that ran from the floor to the ceiling. The third floor was used for storage. Everything was clean and neat, and the floors looked like you could eat off of them. Throughout the house kids were wandering around, looking relaxed and behaving themselves. Things were looking up. The house was in order, and someone knew what he was doing.

But something was missing. I didn't see the director or the staff. When I asked where they were, the judge laughed and took me back downstairs to the kitchen. He pointed to the woman I thought was the cook and said, "Let me reintroduce you. This is Mrs. Sloan, the director, cook, and most of the time the staff." I mumbled something as the judge ushered me out. When we were outside he stopped me on the back porch and gave me some sound advice. He told me to leave the running of the home to Mrs. Sloan, and to concentrate on managing the office. She had been doing it for several years, and he saw no reason for her not to continue.

If logic had anything to do with our society's systems of care, the detention home would have been a disaster area. As I said earlier, we mixed delinquents with neglected children of all ages, and the only staff members other than Mrs. Sloan were her daughters, who would come in as they were needed. One daughter, Betty, was there much of the time and had the same instinctive skills as her remarkable mother. Mrs. Sloan was never told that the job was impossible. She didn't care if her charges were neglected or delinquent. To Mother Sloan they were children, and she could and did nurture all of them. She taught me to ignore the official reports and to look at the child, to look beneath the crusty anger, and to see the real problem. She taught me that most delinquents were neglected children, crying out for help. One night I saw a big, tough sixteen-year-old fight three full-grown policemen to the floor. An hour later he was crying on Mrs. Sloan's shoulder. The next morning the same adolescent was tenderly feeding a baby that had just been brought in.

Mrs. Sloan was a heavyset woman, and wore flower print dresses most of the time. I remember her best standing by the stove. On occasion it seemed as if she was feeding everyone in town. Police, judges, and probation officers all seemed to show up just as Mrs. Sloan was fixing breakfast or lunch. Coveys of children would be hanging on her ever-present apron as she cooked on the big black stove. She once told me that the best say to win the trust of a frightened child was to feed him. "They may reject everything else you have to offer, but they always have to eat."

Most of the children who came in were frightened. She never rushed them. Many of us would try to reach out in our desperate need to provide comfort, but Mrs. Sloan would sit back and allow them to come to her when they were ready. When they did she was there with open arms. She had rules, and the kids knew she was boss, but her structure was as comforting as her hugs.

If I were asked to name the champion nurturer, in my twenty-five years of experience with some of the best in the field, my choice would have to be Mother Sloan. Many of us have the wherewithal to nurture our own, but she took on all comers and did so with a compassion that defied logic. In her I saw the outer limits in a person's capacity to love. With many other parents who were quite knowledgeable about parenting but could not or would not nurture, I have seen children destroyed.

Martin G. was sixteen years old when he committed his first major crime. He singlehandedly trashed his high school. The authorities estimated the damage at $10,000. Martin had thrown the books from the library onto the floor and disconnected the plumbing which, in turn, caused massive flooding, ruining the books. He smashed blackboards, furniture, and windows. The destruction was methodical and diabolical.

I had read about the case in the papers, but had forgotten most of the details when the attorney representing Martin called to ask if I would consider consulting with him and the family. I had just left my work in Chicago, was between jobs, and jumped at the chance. For the better part of two years I had been sitting around big tables thinking big thoughts with lots of big people and had this tremendous need to see the scowling face of a real delinquent.

Martin was everything I could wish for. Some kids like to act like hard cases, but he really was one. When I first saw him, he made no attempt to hide his anger. I sat across from him at the visiting table in the big city detention home and felt the urge to protect my privates. He answered most of my questions with the "F" word, and I walked out convinced that the judge was smart to keep him locked up.

I met the family after I had seen Martin and, as is often the case, was confused by the contrast. The family consisted of a father, Harold, who was an administrator at a university, a mother, Carol, who was a full-time housewife, and three lovely children, all younger than Martin. The attorney and parents were convinced that Martin was simply a "bad seed." I have seen the all-encompassing term "bad seed" used as a cover for problems that most of the family would like to hide. As I have said throughout this book, inappropriate behavior can usually be traced if family members are willing to honestly discuss their feelings and the family history.

There was no question that Martin was the odd man out. His siblings didn't look or act like him. They were good students, and in every way appeared to be as healthy as the parents reported them to be. I asked if Martin was adopted. I asked if there was some kind of trauma surrounding his birth. No, he was theirs, they said, and, no, there was no trauma. The evaluation which included a complete neurological examination, indicated that we were dealing with a very angry young man who was not psychotic or brain damaged.

I would see Martin on a daily basis, and worked with his probation officer and the psychiatrist who had been the team leader in his evaluation. His hostility diminished, but he refused to open up. My time was running out. A new job was waiting, and I was beginning to accept the bad seed theory when his mother, Carol, said something that shed some light. The statement was wedged between other thoughts, and I just about missed it. In essence she said that Martin "looked like that bastard." Carol had been talking about her father and gave a dull description of a blue-collar worker who provided for his family. She had gone on to describe her mother when she threw in the afterthought describing the father. I asked her why her dad was "a bastard." She looked shocked and denied saying it. When I repeated what she said, her face turned red, and she tried again to deny it.

I reported the conversation to the psychiatrist, who, in turn, began to work with her. When it was finally tapped, the story came pouring out. Martin, with his black hair and penetrating blue eyes, did look like his maternal grandfather. The same grandfather who sexually molested his daughter, Carol, from the time she was ten until she left home. She had never told anyone, and the only evidence that it had ever happened was an unconscious act of deprivation.

Martin was the recipient of her hate and anger. She confessed that she treated her eldest differently, but in her honest opinion had never deprived him. Martin's father didn't see the difference between the care Martin received and that which the other children got, but did know that his wife did not like this son. The evolution of this mother's anger and rejection was hard to pinpoint. None of the family members could see that Martin's inappropriate behavior was stimulated by his mother's incapacity to nurture him. For them it was a chicken and egg problem. By the time Martin's mean attitude and angry behavior grew into a daily trial, the whole family was sick of him.

As Carol opened up, she could look back with a whole new perspective. She had not nurtured her son Martin, and she knew the difference. When he suffered a physical injury, she patched the wound but left out the hug. When he was sad, she wasn't. She was a custodial caretaker, not a mother.

It is *not* unusual for one child to be singled out in a family to be "the bad actor." Many of these children are referred to our program, and when they are removed from their natural homes, the parents are often shocked to discover that the family problems and personal problems continue.

I don't know what happened to Carol or Martin, but I do know that I think of Carol first, because she had to work through her trauma before there was much hope for her boy. Both were victims, but if she could have had the insight to realize that her capacity to nurture was not functioning, and sought help, a family disaster could have been avoided.

Some of you reading this book have a deep, dark fear that you do not *like* one or all of your children. When they cry you want to tell them to shut up. When they are afraid, you want to tell them to grow up. When they want hugs, you push them away. If these kind of rejecting feelings seep up from the unconscious, don't hide them and don't run from them. Face them head-on and find out *why* you cannot nurture your own children. Find out why you do not like your kid. It is not natural not to like your child, and if it is a reality, something is wrong that needs to be fixed.

Fixing our capacity to nurture is not as traumatic as we might imagine. In some cases it requires an active reevaluation of your own needs, and in others you might need to get some help to enable you to discover why the resentment exists. We may be talking about some in-depth psychotherapy with a psychiatrist, social worker, or psychologist. There are ministers who are trained to provide professional counseling. If you woke up and your right arm was paralyzed, you would not think twice about calling a doctor. The capacity to nurture is the right arm of parenting.

Carol G. was dealing with a mental block that inhibited her capacity to nurture her son Martin. But more often than not, the motivating force behind the tendency to separate yourself from and become angry at your child is concious, rather than unconcious. For years I have listened to parents and children describe the reasons they do not like each other. The child says he cannot stand his parents because they are cold and uncaring. When you talk to them it is difficult to trace the origins of this conflict, or determine which came first, but the origins are less important than the destructive effects of this interaction.

When we train our family-care parents to assume the responsibility for a new group of children, we tell them that the children will more than likely reject most of their attempts to provide affection. When the parents smile, the child will frown and when the parent touches, the child will pull away. When the child is angry, he just might spit or use hateful, filthy language, or, in some cases, lash out physically.

My advice to these professional parents is the same that I give to natural parents when they find themselves having a hard time loving an unlovable child. "You're the adult. You are the one setting the standard. Continue to provide the affection regardless of the reaction, and don't take their negative response personally. Listen to *what* they say, not the *way* they say it. Look beyond the twisted face and angry words, and see the hurting child, and direct your response to that pain." The parents I have seen who have this capacity are not saints or superhuman, they are people who have learned not to take the angry words and behavior of a volatile child personally. Parents can stop the cycle of anger. I don't say it's easy or pleasant, but in most cases it is a rational solution. Whether you feel like it or not, nurture your child, and the chances are very good that eventually the child will respond positively, and become a lovable human being.

I might add that this advice applies to both mothers and fathers. When we talk of nurturance, all too often the man assumes this is the woman's job. The hugs, the kisses, and the tears of joy and pain need to come from dads and moms.

We seldom read about cases of emotional neglect in the newspaper. We concentrate our concern on physical and sexual abuse. I believe emotional neglect is the number one disease affecting children today. Those children who have not experienced a nurturing relationship with a parent often do not have the capacity to nurture. The result is a destructive domino effect that can wreak havoc for generations.

When our emotional needs for love and security are satisfied, we then have the capacity to give to our children. Adults need to be nurtured as much as children.

When people are divorced, out of work, or experience some other type of disruptive tragedy, they sometimes forget that their own needs are not being met and wonder why their temper is short, and the kid is getting stupid all at once.

When my son Nicholas is tired, hurt, or sick, he will come up to his mother and say he wants "snuggies," which is his way of expressing a need to sit on her lap in the rocking chair, held gently in her arms under a warm blanket. Two weeks before he turned three, Nicholas told

Ginger he did not want to "get big." When she asked why, he said, "Because I can't have snuggies anymore."

It doesn't matter whether we're talking about nurturance or snuggies, we never outgrow our need for it.

10

A child's first and most important teachers are his parents.

Most of what we know about life, what we feel about ourselves, and what we care about is taught by our parents. *You* are your child's teacher and the architect of your child's self-image. But we can easily assume that the school will teach facts, the church will teach morals, the kids comparing notes behind the barn will teach sex, police will teach respect for the law, and television will take care of the rest. Many of us have abdicated our responsibility. Today's parents must not only teach but also monitor what their children are learning if they expect to end up with a well-adjusted adult.

I was in the back of a courtroom and the two people standing in front of me had perplexed, hurt looks on their faces. The father turned to the mother and said, "Where in the world did he learn that?"

They had just heard their fifteen-year-old son say to the judge that he had brutally beaten another boy "because he looked like he was going to hit me and no real man just stands there and takes that."

The phrase he used, "Where in the world did he learn that," is one that I hear often. In this particular case we talked about the possible sources of the child's knowledge. His parents honestly did not know. But when I talked to the boy, he said that he had seen every *Rambo* movie at least three times.

Much of what children know today comes from television, movies, and the popular trends that can and do influence children whose parents leave the education to others. Surveys have documented that children spend more time in front of the television than they do in school. No one has been able to prove that the material they view is harmful to their mental health, but common sense should tell us that most of it is not healthy.

What would you think of a father who runs in from the front yard, yelling for everyone to come out to witness a neighbor beating up his wife? Of course no one would behave so strangely, and to compare that type of behavior with watching TV is unfair. But maybe not. When we allow our kids to view violence in any form for hour after hour, we are condoning it. If I allow my child to eat garbage, she will think that garbage is edible. Our children absorb knowledge from many sources. Are we aware of what they are consuming?

Kids do not function in a vacuum. Their minds are always working, searching for new facts, but they do not have the maturity to discriminate between fact and fiction. You may not want your youngster to learn sex or morals from television, but what have *you* taught them? It is easy to blame the mass media for distorting their perceptions of life, but if we do not provide an alternative we cannot complain.

When our children are babies, most of us take seriously our role as teacher, especially with our firstborn. I will never forget the day I brought my first child, Michael, out of the hospital and put him in the car. I looked down at that beautiful, tiny head covered with three inches of black hair sticking out in every direction and knew that it was time to grow up. Up to that point I had been playing at being a grown-up, but the thought that I was now a father and responsible for this human being who I had created was sobering.

Many of us take this responsibility too seriously. Our first child ends up being the recipient of all of our misbegotten theories on child rearing, and our anxiety is transmitted through our constant vigilance. Parents want their children to be perfect, and worry obsessively about the kid downstairs who crawled two weeks before their own or the little girl in the store who was two months younger than theirs and already walking. The doctor's reassurance that your child is perfectly normal doesn't seem to help. But in spite of our persistent anxiety, the kids survive.

In our society our role as the primary educator of the child from birth to six years of age is fairly well defined. Most of us know without being told or without reading a child development book that we need to teach them to keep their bodies out of the street or the keys out of the light socket. We feel responsible for their ability to walk, talk, or go to the bathroom. We worry about their selfish play habits and plead with them to share.

How and what we teach during this period is important. Our care of the child from birth to six provides the emotional foundation that will affect his behavior throughout his life. We are setting the standard that will affect much of what they think of the world and what they think of themselves. If we turn up our noses and call their body waste dirty while we are potty training, the chances are pretty good the child will feel he is dirty.

It is during this period that children can learn to appreciate books and perceive learning as an adventure. They do not need to be pushed into reading, or counting, but if we read to them with enthusiasm, and talk to them with a healthy respect for their intellect, they will live up to their intellectual capacity.

On the day my youngest child, Nicholas, was born, I vowed to talk to him. If I had a thought, instead of keeping it to myself, I would carry on a conversation with this wobbly-headed baby. The results have been remarkable. Nicholas has an enormous vocabulary, and I believe that any normal child of average intelligence would react the same to intensive verbal exposure.

It is during this period that we teach affection by being affectionate with our spouses, the child's siblings, and the child. Affection and nurturance are taught by example, but it is an essential part of the learning process. Anger and hate can be taught just as effectively if we are not careful.

Self-discipline and the capacity to delay gratification are

ingrained during these formative years. If children live in a willy-nilly household, are never taught to pick up their toys, or are allowed to throw their trash on the floor, the chances are good that they will have a hard time functioning in school or maintaining the self-discipline necessary for work.

On the day your children walk into their kindergarten class they will have established attitudes about people. They won't know the meaning of the word prejudice, but they will have definite ideas as to who is bad and who is good. They will know how to hold grudges, hate, and fear, if that was what they were exposed to at home. Children *learn* a positive or a negative attitude, and they tend to carry whichever reaction process they have adopted for a lifetime.

Children learn about sex and their bodies from us. My son Mark has always been one of those children who has to try everything for himself. He considered forbidden territory a challenge. If you told him not to stick a bean in his ear, Mark would spend two days looking for a bean to stick in his ear. He was three and a half when his mother fixed cherry Jello, without realizing the cherries she had added were not pitted. Luckily she took the first bite, realized the mistake, and warned everyone at the table. "Be careful. Don't swallow the cherry seeds." Fatal words to a curious Mark. Within seconds he had swallowed one, and proceeded to panic. We asked if it was stuck in his throat. He said no. We assured him that it would be all right, but he wouldn't let go. "Where is the cherry seed? Am I gonna die?" We told him it would now pass through his body and not to worry. All evening and sporadically over the next month, Mark would ask about the seed. Six weeks passed and we had just put the kids to bed and settled down for the first relaxing moment alone with the newspaper. Mark came stumbling out of his bedroom, with his pajama bottoms at his ankles, and, holding one of his testicles, said, "I found it, I found the cherry seed."

The point is that when our children begin to explore their bodies and ask questions, we need to think about how we answer. The how is more important than the actual words. If we turn up our nose and look disgusted at the question about the penis or vagina, they understand immediately how we feel. By then whatever words we choose are virtually meaningless. They will ask questions and be curious. For the better part of two years we cover their bodies with diapers, and when finally they have a chance to explore and discover these strange organs, they will be fascinated and excited. I once had a young mother tell me that her eighteen-month-old child was already showing signs of being a sexual pervert. When she described a little boy holding on to, and playing with his penis, I told her that his behavior was normal, but if she was uptight about sexual matters, it would soon affect him. Her concern would become a self-fulfilling prophesy.

Out of one side of my mouth I say that young parents are often too uptight about the first years of their child's life, and out of the other propose this horrendous list of parental responsibilities. But we do take the formative years seriously, and most young parents do a fine job of meeting these familial expectations.

The problem that I see starts after the sixth birthday. It is then that we send them off to school and have a tendency to forget that our job is just beginning.

Do you ever think about how well prepared your child

is to enter the world? Are you sitting back thinking that you will wait until your children are eighteen or twenty to see what kind of product the school system turned out? In the Menninger Youth Program we think about these questions all the time. The children we get have been deprived socially and educationally. Many of them don't know how to eat with knives, forks, or spoons. We get teenagers who don't know how to read or complete simple math problems. Some cannot make change or tell time. They are socially retarded, and we have a short time to cram in the basic information they need to survive in a world that can be cruel to those who are ill prepared.

For each child we create a treatment plan. First we evaluate his current level of abilities. We take a look at his educational skills, social skills, hygiene habits, ability to function with peers, capacity to take direction, relate to adults, or relate to authority figures. This working document is referred to weekly and updated every three months. If the child can't read, we get a tutor. If he can't hear, we get a hearing aid or operation; if he gets angry every time someone asks him to do something, we develop a plan to address the problem. That plan may include psychotherapy or working one on one with a kindly old bricklayer. These plans, and the resulting strategies for resolution, are as varied as the individuals being considered.

We go back to the basics. We teach them how to answer the phone and meet strangers at the front door. We teach them table and telephone manners. By the time they leave, our children know how to introduce their friends to other people, and look people in the eye when they shake hands.

Most parents have already taught their children these

essentials, but they are the tip of the iceberg, and you might begin to think about what your child does and does not know.

None of us are perfect parents who teach our children everything they need to know, but you can be logical and evaluate your child's strengths and weaknesses. Once you have identified them, you can then support the strengths and develop a plan to deal with the weaknesses. As you do so, you may need support and advice from friends, family, or even professionals. Don't worry about being embarrassed. Most of your friends and family will admire your ability to accept and deal with your child's shortfalls.

The following is a checklist that may be useful as you evaluate your child's strengths and weaknesses.

EDUCATIONAL NEEDS

Skill levels in reading, writing, and math

Just because your child is bringing home passing grades doesn't mean he knows how to read, write, or add. Study his textbooks to determine appropriate skill levels, and develop your own tests. Sit down with him and have him read out loud. Devise some math problems and ask him to solve them. Have your child write grandmother a letter, with the understanding that you will read it. Your expectations may be higher than the educational systems, and you might be shocked by your child's performance. If you find shortcomings, you need to take action. This action on your part may include tutors, teaching him yourself, and informing the school that you expect more from them.

Anger at the student or the school system is counter-productive.

Peer interaction

When you ask him how things went at school today, and he smiles and says "great," chances are he isn't talking about what he learned. Children, especially adolescents, judge the quality of their days by how well they relate with their peers. It is important for you to know how your child gets along with the other kids, even though nothing hurts more than to discover he is excluded from the group he wants to belong to, or has been labeled "nerd," "thug," "stupid," or "egghead." Just knowing the status of these relationships can help you understand your child's behavior at home. Parents aren't helpless in these circumstances. Children develop relationships primarily through activities. You can't find your child friends, but you can guide him to special activities where he can succeed. Nothing draws friends faster than success. You may also discover that your child does have irritating personality traits that need to be corrected. We can't always blame everyone else.

Who are his friends? How does he relate to them?

Ability to follow directions

How well does he follow directions at home? Have you had complaints from school? Have you asked how he responds to directions at school? Does he have the capacity to follow directions in the subjects he likes, but not in the classes that bore him? Learning to follow directions is a skill that can be taught and that he will use throughout his life.

Attention span

Can he sit still and listen to a story, or read a book? Can you carry on a conversation with him and expect him to stay with you to the conclusion? If you discover he has a short attention span and is unable to concentrate long enough to learn, there are solutions. Children do have the ability to improve their concentration. A child with a short attention span, through various exercises, can be conditioned to keep his mind on the subject at hand. Start with something simple. If he can't sit still more than five minutes, develop a game. Ask him to think of something pleasant, and see if he can sit still for ten minutes. Give him a reward if he does. The next day extend the time, and give him a simple phrase to learn while he sits.

Intellectual capacity

Does he ask questions when he is curious? Does he have a variety of interests, or spend more of his time staring at cartoons on television? Do you answer the questions he asks? Do you take him to the local zoo, or museums? Do members of your family read out loud to each other when something of interest is found in the paper? The brain is a muscle that needs exercise as much as any other part of the body.

Self-starting capacity

Does he do his homework without your prodding? Do you have to beg him to complete a chore? Does he begin a self-designed project, and follow through?

Leadership potential

Can he convince his friends or family members to follow his lead? Does he respond when someone asks which
movie to go to? Does he consider his opinions important?
Does he always need to be with friends to be happy?

Frustration tolerance

How does he react when you ask him to complete tasks?
If he is stumped on a math problem, how does he solve it?
Is he willing to take on challenging games, or puzzles?

Self-discipline

Do you have to remind him to complete such tasks as
making the bed, or cleaning his room? Do you have to
send him to bed, and beg him to get up in the morning?

If you sit down with your child's teachers and school
counselors and ask these questions and any other questions you want to add, you may be surprised at the
amount of information you come away with. The following checklists suggest additional questions to ask yourself.

PHYSICAL/MEDICAL/DENTAL NEEDS

Hygiene

How hard is it to get him to wash his face, take a
shower, brush his teeth, keep his hair clean? There are
times when he will be telling you how he feels inside by
neglecting his appearance. Most children go through an
"I'm too busy to care how I look" phase, but if it continues

through mid- or late-adolescence, it could be a symptom of other problems.

Speech

Can you understand what he is saying? Does he have a lisp or stutter? The lisp may be cute when he is young, but it can be a detriment when he grows older. Speech therapists can do wonders with most problems.

Hearing

Does he ask you to repeat your statements when you talk to him? Does he turn up the radio or television when everyone else in the room is able to hear at a moderate volume? Doctors have issued warnings to parents and children that the loud music blasting through the earphones or portable radios can cause hearing loss.

Eating problems

Has he stopped eating? Does he talk and think about food compulsively? Have you noticed a radical weight loss or gain? Does he eat when he is upset? Does he binge and then go to the bathroom? Eating disorders have become a modern scourge, and the number of boys and girls fighting this problem is rising at an alarming rate. Consult your doctor and ask for information on eating disorders. It is an addictive behavior, and can be lethal.

Sleep habits

Does he get up at all hours of the night? Is it difficult to get him out of bed? This can be a sign of depression. Sleep disorders are symptoms that need to be taken seriously.

Exercise habits

Is he a couch potato? Does he run every morning and night, and get upset when his routine is disrupted? Both extremes are dangerous to his health.

SOCIAL SKILLS

Does he have friends and interact with a variety of people? Has he started associating with the children in school who are considered rebels?

Does he dress appropriately, or does he put on the wildest thing he can find?

Does he have appropriate telephone and table manners?

Does he demonstrate self-confidence in public places while meeting new people?

Does he make direct eye contact when he talks to you or others?

Does his behavior change radically when he is in the presence of girls?

Does he become nervous or defensive when confronted by authority? Does he rebel at every request or submit willingly to any and all commands? Either extreme is cause for concern. Can he tolerate stress? Does he flunk tests when he knows the answers?

Is he aware of himself? Is he aware that there is a physical and emotional self?

Does he know how to express what he is thinking? Are there good thoughts going to waste because he simply can't get them out?

Has he demonstrated a capacity for self-control, or does he become hysterical in situations when hysteria is not called for? Does he have any hobbies? Is he a one-dimensional person without fallback interests to occupy his time in a healthy, enjoyable way?

Does he have any recreational skills? Everyone doesn't need to be an athlete, but you need to teach your child how to have fun and exercise his body.

Does he know how to delay gratification? Or does he want what he wants when he wants it?

At the Menninger Youth Program, we don't set up treatment plans because our kids are crazy; we set up treatment plans because we need to prepare them to go into the world and function as confident adults. We know that the job market is more competitive than at any time in the last fifty years. Employers who offer decent jobs don't need to put up with poorly qualified, irresponsible employees.

I am asking you to think about doing the same for your child. I hate to see parents shocked when their eighteen-year-old child with a high school diploma confesses he can't fill out the job application because he can't read.

I went to a wedding party several months ago and watched a mother cry as her son, the groom, struggled with introductions, and then inadvertently made a fool of himself as he violated most of the rules of table etiquette. He wasn't showing off, drunk, or being rebellious; he was socially ignorant. His parents weren't, but he was.

The following is a simplified example of just how an improvement plan was used by a young couple. Mr. and Mrs. H. had three healthy boys. They were gregarious, active, and at times too aggressive, but generally, they were thought to be normal. The oldest son, Kirby, started school on time and proceeded without a hitch. The middle one, Kent, started school a year later and everything seemed to be fine until Mr. and Mrs. H. were called in near the end of the school year and told that he was not learning. He didn't know his alphabet, was having trouble learning math concepts, and spent much of his time sucking his thumb or being disruptive. By the end of the year they again confronted the school and were told their boy would need to repeat the first grade.

They developed their own improvement plan. They hired a tutor, set up a study time, and for several months of the next year they kept in daily contact with the teacher. The plan worked and the young boy came out of his dull behavior, and proceeded to become an average but perfectly adequate student. His parents did not panic or saddle their child with guilt and the repeating of the first grade was never interpreted as a failure. Poor Kent didn't understand that he had failed until years later.

Mr. and Mrs. H. happen to be my parents. At that point in my life they could have done several things that could have seriously damaged an impressionable young ego. But they maintained their faith in me, and continually conveyed their confidence. Their plan was simple, but it was effective.

If we do not actively monitor our children's progress and think through solutions to problems as they arise, we are custodians, not parents.

Jessie was fifteen years old when she was referred to one of our demonstration projects. It was 1969, and we had just put our new treatment plan into effect. She was going to be one of the first participants in the new program and, after reviewing her case history, we knew we would need every tool we could put our hands on.

Jessica Lynn V. was abandoned when she three. Since that time she had been placed in seventeen foster homes, retained in the juvenile detention center on nine separate occasions, and undergone four complete psychiatric evaluations. All four evaluations said the same thing. Once we were able to interpret the psychiatric jargon, the diagnosis and resulting conclusions were simple: Jessie was an angry, insecure child in need of a stable home environment. There was a note attached to the bottom of the final document that was addressed to the state worker who had requested the evaluation. "Do not evaluate this child again. The problem is not in her it is in your fucked-up system that is slowly destroying her." The worker had obviously not taken the time to read the report, otherwise he would have removed the note.

She was five feet two, one hundred fifty-seven pounds, with a pasty white complexion and pimples. Her angry expression was partly obscured by a wild mass of straight brown hair. She had a homemade tatoo on her left shoulder that spelled out JESSIE in primitive, jagged lettering. On her left hip she had tattooed the names Mary and John. The oldest case summary said her parents' names may have been Mary and John.

She had run away from the latest foster home three months earlier, and survived on the streets by prostitution and by running errands for the local drug pusher. She was willing to come to our home because the judge had given her the choice of going to our program or the state reform school. All things considered, you would have thought she would have been more than happy to move into our brand new $150,000 home, but Jessie let it be known from the moment our people sat down at the first interview that she was coming because she had no choice. She didn't want our "Goody two shoes handouts, and if you goddamned people helpers would leave me alone, I would be fine."

The staff came back from this interview convinced that we would be butting our heads into a brick wall. The prognosis for success was grim. The family-care parents were not responsible for making the decision, but I had known Liz and Kurt long enough to trust their instincts. I asked one question: "Do you think we have a ghost of a chance?" Liz and Kurt smiled at each other, shrugged their shoulders, and said, "Why not?" Now that I think back, that was their answer every time I asked it.

We had the information we needed to develop an initial treatment plan, and as was the policy, we formulated the first draft before the child was admitted. Through this exercise, the family-care parents and support staff know what issues we want to deal with, and how.

Jessie was reading and writing at the fourth-grade level, but her math skills were on par with her age group. Two of the other children in the house were responding to a young tutor, but Jessie hated most men, and he was young and inexperienced. We decided to give him a try, but to monitor her progress and switch to a new tutor at the first sign of trouble. Our social worker agreed to talk to the young man and explain the circumstance. He was a good volunteer, and we did not want the success he was having with the other two girls to be disrupted because of a blowup with Jessie.

She was almost sixteen and was classified as an eighth grader, but had not been in school for most of the previous year. We agreed to put her in the eighth grade as a full-time student, but to go to half days if she showed signs of breaking out. Our school coordinator went to the school and worked out the treatment plan and curriculum with the special education staff.

Jessie hated adults. We knew of two occasions when she had accused foster fathers of sexually molesting her. These allegations were never proven, and there was no way of finding out if that had occurred. Kurt was advised to limit the times when he was alone with her. The incidents pointed to her fear of men, and we would need to respect that fear. She was able to tell us later that one of the foster fathers had in fact raped her, and she used the rape charge against the other one to get out of the home. It was the consensus of the group that if she ever settled in the home we would enlist the help of a psychotherapist.

We chose her roommate carefully. We wanted someone strong enough to withstand her initial resistance and anger, and someone who could identify with her background and problems. Julie was seventeen, and had been in the program eighteen months. She was sold by her mother as a prostitute when she was ten, and had given birth to a boy when she was fourteen. Julie had settled into the program, but still had enough of a street-tough mentality to impress Jessie.

Every other word out of Jessie's mouth was "fuck" as well as a rich variety of other four-letter words. In one of the later additions to her plan, Liz started a program in which Jessie was paid for every day she got through without cursing. One day Liz walked from the house to the small pond over the hill and saw Jessie staring at the water and saying every curse word she could think of. Liz never told her, and Jessie got her money that day.

When Jessie was settled we set up a weight and exercise program that she resisted in a halfhearted way. She went to a skin specialist and learned how to wash her face and care for her complexion.

Jessie simultaneously begged for and complained about the structures Liz and Kurt set for her, but within ten months it became obvious that she had bonded with them. The treatment plan shifted, and we began to expect specific results.

The state would allow us to care for this child until she was eighteen years old, but after that she was out on the streets again. She had no relatives, and other than us, there was no support system. She was in the ninth grade and quickly approaching her seventeenth birthday. We didn't panic, but at the same time we knew the importance of preparing Jessie to survive.

It would be impossible for me to remember everything we put in Jessie's treatment plan, but it seemed to work. She was impressed with the house and later she told us how much it meant that it was built for her and that she was not sharing someone else's home. The bedspread that she and Liz had picked out the second day of her stay is now on the wall of her bedroom. She says it is her most prized possession.

Once she was convinced that this home was secure she made remarkable progress. We provided the strategy, but Jessie had to do the work. Kurt compared the treatment plan to all the king's horsemen putting Humpty Dumpty back together again. One painful step at a time, we helped this child deal with her own shortfalls. It was a methodical but caring process.

Through a special agreement with the state, we were able to keep Jessie until she was nineteen and graduated from high school. On the night of her graduation, I could not believe that this beautiful, dignified young woman walking across the stage was our Jessie. The acne was gone, the back was straight, head held high, hair shining, but most importantly she was a whole person. Jessie was ready to go into the world and meet it on her own terms.

She is now married and is an executive with a computer firm.

All of us want to take shortcuts and say things like "Why don't those kids behave themselves? Maybe they need treatment, or medicine, or punishment." *We want one simple, clean answer,* but there is no magic solution. The answers are multiple, and the solution requires planning and commitment.

As your child's primary educator, you need to design the curriculum. Find out what excites your child and develop a hobby or create work projects or exercise programs. As we evaluate the content of our children's learning, we need to look at what they pick up from our behavior. What do they think about authority figures when we talk about that "stupid cop who gave me a ticket"? What do they learn when they hear us joke at other people's expense, or use bigoted slang?

It is sometimes frightening to look down into those eager little faces and watch the alert eyes, absorbing everything they see. Have you ever asked yourself the questions: "What do I want my children to know before they leave home?" "Have I given them the knowledge to function in that world out there?"

11

*Good parents teach their children
that there is joy in being part
of a larger community.*

"Who knows what evil lurks in the hearts of men?" These
were the opening lines of "The Shadow," a great old radio
mystery show. The deep, rich voice would drone out the
frightening phrase each week, and a little chill would
feather the back of my neck as I imagined the lurking evil
and the dreadful people just outside my front door waiting
to pounce upon my little bones. But except for these titillating escapes into a scary fantasy, I didn't worry much
about what went on outside our unlocked front door. I
grew up in small towns, and didn't know about real evil.

Our communities were safe places, and my parents taught me to believe in the basic goodness of people. That is how I was introduced to the world outside my immediate family.

Before your children get out of diapers, they begin to look out the front window, pointing to the garbage truck, the mailman, or the paper boy, asking who they are and where they fit into their world. How you introduce your child to the world is important.

As I studied the cases of the upper-class criminal I have worked with, I began to see a pattern of family behavior that I had never before recognized as a common causative agent. like a detective reevaluating existing clues in a search for new leads, I went back to see what I had missed. And in over 50 percent of the cases, I found a problem that was consistently present.

The parents of children who grow up rebellious and angry teach them, by word and deed, that you cannot trust other people. The parents of criminals, more often than not, have few friends or relationships with their extended families. They do not trust their neighbors, their community leaders, their police force, and in many cases, other members of their extended family. They create an atmosphere of paranoid isolation within the home.

When these circumstances exist, children begin to have a "we-they" mentality. "We" includes everyone within the four walls of their home, and "they" encompasses the rest of society. With this mindset, it is easy to understand the delusional thinking that often accompanies delinquent behavior: "If they are out to screw me, then I have the right to screw them first."

Most of you reading this material will now relax, thinking you can go on to the next chapter because this issue does not concern you. But before you do, think about some of the messages that you pass on to your children. We live in a society that often causes anger and stress, and in the grip of these emotions we may pass on messages to our children that we do not really believe.

A friend told me about his two-year-old who would sit next to him in the front seat of the car, point his finger at the other drivers, and say, "asshole." The child had learned from his father's angry words that other drivers were "assholes," and angry words make more of an impression on young minds than do rational statements.

Each night on the national news we get an updated report on the number of shootings on the Los Angeles freeways. We can no longer discount the stress of living in overpopulated cities. It does have an impact on your children's perceptions of the world they live in.

For the past few years we have gotten swept up in a mass public hysteria. We have been told that hundreds of thousands of children have been abducted, raped, and killed. That "strangers" lurking behind every bush and waiting next to every school yard are out to take our young ones. Mass media educational campaigns have been launched to teach our children not to trust strangers. What we are now learning is that the number of actual abductions by strangers was grossly exaggerated. Most of these abductions are by ex-spouses, not strangers, and most of the "missing children" are runaways.

Unfortunately, the emotional backlash from this hysterical reaction will take years to correct. Many children now believe that anyone they do not know is automatically bad. When I was a child, I felt a titillating excitement while listening to "The Shadow" talk about evil. My parents would give me a hug, and tell me that it's just a show. Children today are being told that the evil is real, and is just around every corner.

Obviously, I teach my children not to get into cars with people they don't know, but I refuse to condemn each and every human who does not know me. We are creating prisons of fear for our children. Looking at the actual statistics, the chances of my child being abducted are infinitesimal, but if I teach him to distrust all strangers, the chances are great that I will take away from him one of life's greatest joys: meeting a new friend.

When we go out, my son Nicholas says "Hi" to everyone. We were in the grocery store recently, and as our cart passed another one with a child perhaps a year older, Nicholas reached out, touched the boy's arm, and said, "Hi." The child pulled back looked at his mother, and said, "Is he a stranger?" Without looking at my child, or taking the time to think, she said, "Yes, dear, he is a stranger." I would not try to imagine the limited concept of community that this child will have.

Regardless of the mother's attempt to protect him, her boy will soon be exposed to "strangers," but will do so with no social skills, training, and no capacity to determine the difference between people who could be dangerous and those who are there to help. With her definition of "stranger," her child will distrust the crossing guard his first day of school, and who knows how long it will take for his teacher to be eliminated from the category.

These negative notions that we are passing along to our children can be counterbalanced by positive interactions with friends and members of the community. Children must be taught through social interaction that they are a part of a larger community and that the maintenance of the larger community is their responsibility. They learn how to be social by watching their parents socialize.

I was the second son of a Methodist minister. My father and mother taught me, by their example, to trust and love people. During the Second World War they took a Japanese girl, whose parents had been placed in one of the internment camps, into our home. When many people were convinced that all Japanese were dangerous spies, I was learning otherwise. When the hobos came through town, they knew that our house was a place where they could get a free meal. My brothers and I would sit and talk for hours with these fascinating men. When problems arose in the community, our whole family jumped into the fray. I learned that if you have a community problem, the only way to solve it is by getting involved. If we as parents allow our fears to isolate us from the community at large, we risk the emotional well-being of our children.

Our children are imitators. The chances are good that they will associate with the same type of people we associate with. If we are loners, our children will probably be loners. Our mistrust will become their mistrust.

Ted M. first came to the court's attention on a charge of assault when he was fourteen years old. He had cornered a teacher and struck her several times with a heavy yardstick. The teacher was surprised by the behavior, and was unsure about signing a complaint. I was present when Ted's parents arrived at the detention home. Dr. M. and his wife looked like the successful people they in fact were. He was tall and thin, and had an air of superiority that included a particular look down his sharp, aristocratic nose.

Ted was sitting in the detention-home office when his parents walked in. The superior air vanished as father and son embraced immediately, and his mother cried into her husband's shoulder. After some mumbled explanations from boy to father, we separated them. The boy's probation officer talked to him, and I took the parents into the living room. They were baffled by Ted's behavior, and assured me that they would get to the bottom of the problem immediately.

The probation officer said Ted felt the teacher was treating him unfairly by having him stay after school, and he lost his temper, but he would never do it again. We released Ted to the custody of the parents, and two hours later the teacher called to withdraw the complaint. I doubted that we would ever see the boy again because too many good things were in place. The child and parents had what appeared to be a good and nurturing relationship, and the boy was bright and articulate.

Later that same evening I returned to the detention home on other business. Mrs. Sloan, the detention home director, asked what happened with Ted. I told her and started to walk away. She said she didn't feel right about that boy. I stopped in my tracks and returned for an explanation. Mrs. Sloan could read kids better than any person I have met. When she said she didn't feel right, I listened. I had seen some of the biggest, meanest-looking thugs in town come through that place, and when I would comment on how bad they must be, she would laugh. Within days she would have them cleaned up and behaving like gentlemen. This time she couldn't define her concern. The boy had not demonstrated his anger, or any form of unruly behavior in her presence, but she felt something brewing in this child that was not healthy, and wanted to let me know. I can remember getting in the car and thinking that Mrs. Sloan couldn't be right all the time, and this was one of those times.

Three months passed, and I had forgotten about Ted and Mrs. Sloan's dire prediction when the phone next to my bed rang. The police were at the detention home with a fifteen-year-old boy by the name of Ted M. and his irate father. Ted had assaulted a fifteen-year-old friend, and according to eyewitness accounts, he would have killed the boy if the other boys present had not pulled him off. Ted's father was threatening to sue the police, the juvenile court, and everyone else involved if they did not release the boy to his custody.

I got out of bed and went to the detention home. It was twelve-thirty in the morning. Ted was sitting quietly in the office, Mrs. Sloan was fixing the officers coffee, and the father was smiling confidently, now that someone in authority had come to release his son. I told him I needed to talk to the police and Ted and then we would talk. He said that it was late, he had hospital rounds early the next morning, and I could get the information from Ted in the morning. I told the man as diplomatically as possible that he could go home but Ted would spend the night in detention. He huffed and puffed, but eventually went in to say goodbye to his son and left. Ted would not talk to me. After several failed attempts to communicate with the boy, we placed him in a single cell on the second floor.

Around ten o'clock the next morning, Ted's probation officer came into tell me the boy Ted had assaulted was now out of critical condition, but was left with a crushed cheekbone, broken nose, and smashed kneecap. Ted would not talk to his probation officer or the police. I decided to go over and give it a try.

Like his father, Ted was tall and wiry. He had big hands, squared-off shoulders, and a physical maturity that belied his fifteen years. I opened his cell door, and went in to sit next to him on his bunk. He stared at the wall, refusing to answer any of my questions. When it became obvious he was not going to talk, I stood, closed the door made of open bars, and started to walk away. I was about four steps from the cell when I felt a sharp object skim my neck just below my left ear. I stood staring at the homemade spear lodged in a door twenty feet in front of my face, quivering from the impact, before I realized that it was the cause of the stinging pain and blood on my neck. I turned slowly and looked into a pair of cold, dark brown eyes. Ted's blank expression didn't change for several seconds, and then a slow smile began to bend his mouth. The eyes didn't change.

We never did find out how he got the mop handle in the cell, and since he would not talk, we assumed he had sharpened it on the rough cement floor. Ted had no intention of escaping; I had already locked his door. He simply wanted to kill me.

Over the next several weeks he was talked to by every expert money could buy, given brain scans, and hypnotized, but no one was willing to say they knew, absolutely, what his problem was. After much thought the judge agreed to allow him to be hospitalized in a secure environment. The facility was in upstate New York, and I didn't expect ever to see Ted M. again. The psychiatrists who were willing to venture a guess said he was probably a chronic schizophrenic who would be hospitalized most of his life.

In the introduction of this book I said I could usually sit down with a family and, with enough information, diagnose the cause of a child's wayward behavior. But this case stumped me. The only explanation seemed to be the chemical imbalance that was thought to be the primary factor in chronic schizophrenia.

Several years passed and I was sitting in my office when my secretary buzzed to say an old friend had stopped by to say hello. I didn't ask who it was but simply stood and went to the outer office. I tried to produce a convincing smile as I looked again into those dark brown eyes. He was grown up, and looked like Tom Selleck. As far as I could see, there was no malice or anger on the handsome face, but the itch behind my left ear was hard to suppress.

Ted said he had thought of me often, and, after several years in the hospital, found it hard to believe he had thrown the mop handle at my head. He had this need to see me to make sure I was all right. We talked of other things, and when it became obvious I was conversing with a sane, rational person, I confessed my ignorance in his case. I told Ted that I felt there was something that I or his probation officer had missed. Why had this bright young man gone off the deep end? He told me that if I had the time he would tell me what he had learned during his four years in the hospital.

We talked for three hours, and I listened as he told me what it was like living with an angry man. Ted's father apparently hated the world, but in public the only clue was his rigid, aloof exterior. At home he raved about the ridiculous school system, stupid cops, and crazy neighbors, and he would encourage Ted when he complained about other people's treatment of him. One of the few ways Ted could get his father's attention was to reveal to him a new indignity imposed by one of those idiots outside their home. "My teacher is picking on me because I'm ahead of the other kids in reading. She made me pick up the books." Whereas the father had the maturity to turn off his antisocial attitude outside the home, Ted could not. On the night I told Dr. M. to go home, and put Ted in a cell, his father told him I was out to get him, and they would have to take care of me. That thought worked on Ted all night in the lonely cell, and by the time I came the next morning, he was prepared to carry out his father's intent.

Ted believed that the world was a bad place, and that his father was one of the few good things in it. He was frightened most of the time, because he believed the cops were out to get him and his family. Eventually he turned on his lifelong friends. His father had told him that these young people were avoiding him and trying to leave him out. His friends were out to get him. Ted's father had taught a philosophy of paranoia, and like most good and obedient children, Ted had obeyed his father. His mother committed suicide, and his father left his home two years ago and has not been seen since. Ted had one older sister who had taken him under her wing and understood better than any of us the reason for his behavior. The sister thought her father had joined a neo-Nazi group somewhere in the Northwest.

It was Ted's eloquent description of his family that made me begin to take more seriously the notion that many children exhibiting angry behavior are, in fact, acting out their parents' antisocial attitudes. I should explain that I am not talking about the thief who teaches his child to steal, but about respected people who fail to interact with others in the community. I am talking about people who fail to teach their children to respect the rights and dignity of others.

Your children need to feel the security that can only come when they experience true participation in the community. I know there are people on the streets who are selling dope and molesting children, but for every one of them there are thousands of decent, loving people ready and waiting to be their friends and protectors. Everyone knows that there are risks involved in climbing a mountain, but you have a choice of assuming that risk or avoiding the mountain.

Most of the children who come to our projects are shy and withdrawn. Many act tough in the house, but know they are safe there. They have learned from hard experience that the street is a mean place to be. We don't push too fast, but eventually we encourage them to venture out. Their primary fear is of being rejected in this new, well-to-do environment, which I might add is the same reason most of us fail to participate in community activities. These swank treelined streets seem to them like forbidden territory, and they believe they will never fit in with people who are successful. We have to break down the "we-they" mentality they have been taught from birth.

We get them involved in a church of their choice, a youth group, or a special interest group. In most cases the children accompany the family-care parents as the parents pursue their hobbies or religious faith. But, more impor-

tant, we encourage them to volunteer their time at the
local hospital or some other nonprofit facility.

Not long ago, I was walking down the street in Boston
when someone touched my arm. I instinctively pulled
back, but immediately realized my error as I looked into
the beautiful face of the young woman who had reached
out. She asked if I recognized her. I confessed ignorance,
but saw something familiar. When she told me her name, I
found it hard to believe it was the same child I had known.
I had forty minutes, and she was on her noon break, so we
decided to have lunch. The forty minutes whizzed by as
we tried desperately to fill in the gaps.

The last time I remembered seeing Jackie she was fifteen years old, pimply faced, overweight, and angry at the
world. She had come to one of the family-care homes in
the first demonstration project I had founded just as I was
leaving to start another project. She had had a baby, was
on drugs, was picked up in an armed robbery, and hated
the world and everyone in it. If I remember right, that
included me. She confirmed my memory. Her chances of
success were slim, and the family-care mother accused me
of going to a new job just to get away from this hellcat I
had dropped at her doorstep. Deb and Bob were wonders
in their own right, and I had seen some certifiable miracles come out of their broods, but I did feel guilty about
leaving this new girl.

Jackie said it was hard and the parents were patient, but
for several months she felt like a useless outsider. When
Deb or Bob would try to build her up, she would tell them
they were stupid for believing in her and proceed to tear
down whatever they were trying to build. One day Deb
ran in, grabbed her by the hand, and said there was an

emergency at the hospital: One of the other girls in the home who was doing volunteer work was sick and Jackie would have to fill in. She protested, but by that time they were in the car and were halfway to the hospital. It worked. This beautiful, composed young woman sat across from me in a small restaurant in Boston and told me what that simple volunteer job had meant to her. Jackie said people had been trying to help her all her life, but when she realized that she was capable of helping someone else, she found something of value in herself. She felt like she was part of the community when she realized that she could be a productive participant.

Your children need to experience the same kind of involvement, and you need to guide that participation.

Certain kinds of activities lend themselves to family interaction. I have told you about my son Mark, the horse trainer. He has the grandest variety of friends, people from every walk of life, and their common interest is horses. This avocation brings together bartenders, plumbers, doctors, secretaries, politicians, and dogcatchers, but once they don their boots they are just horse people.

Several months ago he bought a new place but the existing barn was inadequate, and he said he was going to build a new one himself. I didn't say anything, but I did not in my wildest imagination believe he could build his own barn. What I didn't take into account was that his friends would get together and help him. In three weeks he had a twelve-stall barn. My brother and I then went out to help install the roof. No one was quite sure how it should be done, but one of the professional men present took charge and began to supervise the process.

About that time Cecil, an older cowboy who everyone

seemed to know, showed up. He listened to the self-appointed foreman for several minutes. Finally he yelled at Mark, "Mark, can I talk now?" Everyone shut up, and Mark said that, yes, Cecil could talk. "Well, Mark, this old Jack [the person trying to supervise the construction] is a fine gentleman and a real scholar, but when it comes to roofs, he's the type that could screw up a one-house paper route." Everyone laughed, including Jack, who quickly turned the job over to Cecil.

These good people gave up their free time to build a barn for a friend, but they enjoyed being a part of a group of people that cared for one another. Mark's and Suzie's babies, my two granddaughters, Jolene and Tiffany, will grow up secure in the knowledge that they are an active part of the community in which they live.

12

*Parents who learn the facts
about alcohol and drug addiction
are their child's greatest allies
against the danger of substance abuse.*

Ninety percent of the people in this country will be or
have been touched personally by addiction. Like me, they
have stared at the phone at three in the morning, waiting
for it to ring, yet hoping it would not. I have experienced
the anguish and helplessness of watching a loved one being destroyed by alcohol. As a person who has lived
through it and won, the following suggestions are the result of a great deal of thought, prayer, and experience.

What can we do?

Some have concluded that peer pressure is the answer.

They argue that kids need to govern their own behavior and look down on those who take drugs or drink excessively. Drug use should be made unpopular through educational campaigns. Once they decide that getting high is not the "in" thing, they will stop buying, and if there is no demand, the supply will go away. The concept is valid, but this is not the definitive answer.

In our desperate search for a solution to this seemingly unsolvable problem, we have the tendency to ignore the people who have the greatest ability to influence a child's behavior: parents. Mothers and fathers who are willing to take the necessary steps can have an impact. There will be parents reading this who have done everything humanly possible to stop their children from using abusive drugs, and who scoff at my optimism. As a person directly involved, I understand the meaning of the word helpless and can identify with the frustration of embattled parents. But after four years of struggle, and eventual recourse to a successful treatment program, I did learn how, as a parent, I could have had an impact and perhaps cut short the extended trauma that affected our whole family.

I can see now how I aided the addiction. In the beginning, I did not recognize or ignored the signs, hoping against hope that the drinking would go away. And even once the addiction had been openly discussed, I supported the habit by becoming the person who assumed the responsibility for this person's drinking. I was the *enabler,* a term that substance abuse treatment people give to the relative or friend who assumes responsibility for the usage. I was using all of my tried and true caring instincts, but when it came to addiction, those instincts backfired.

What does work?

We can start by setting an example. I cannot think of a problem about which we as a society are more hypocritical than drug use. We often delegate the responsibility for monitoring our children's involvement to other agencies because of our need to deny our own addictions and the role they play in encouraging our youngsters to partake. We live in a pleasure-oriented society, and if we come home from work and are not having fun, we feel we deserve a high. If adults believe that sailing a ship or climbing a mountain requires a can of beer to make it entertaining, why shouldn't our children believe the same? Children learn from what they see, not what they hear. If they see a parent who can only relax with a drink in his or her hand, what does it say? Parents need to analyze their own consumption habits. They need to think about the way they act in front of their children when they are drinking, and when they are not.

As a society we need to think about the examples we set, and the images we create. The male heroes in many movies and books are two-fisted drinkers. In my formative years I grew up in a home that was totally abstinent. I don't think my brothers or I ever saw a can of beer or a bottle of wine in our refrigerator. But the men I admired in the books I devoured were called real men and drank voluminous quantities of hard liquor.

Today's youth are confronted with even more confusing misinformation. Their rock star heroes brag of their drug consumption and compose songs describing the euphoria of getting high. It should be noted that some of these same stars have reached bottom, received treatment, and have come back to tell their stories. We can only hope our children listen.

Parents need to assume the responsibility of being their child's drug educator. You could start by going to or contacting the nearest office of the National Council on Alcoholism, where you will find a rich variety of free pamphlets and reading lists. The material includes information on marijuana, cocaine, and other addictive substances, including alcohol. You will learn the terms, the types of drugs available, and the warning signs that will help you intercede early if your child is using them. Like me, you will learn that once your loved one is addicted you will have to repress some of your nurturing and parenting instincts, to force him into a position in which he realizes that he must help himself. This task is possible without becoming sarcastic or vindictive.

You will acquire a working knowledge of the shocking statistics on substance abuse that will motivate you to sit down with your child and tell him about the risks involved. In 1985, the National Council on Alcoholism stated that 100,000 ten- and eleven-year-olds reported getting drunk at least once a week. Even six-year-olds need to be talked to. But how do you talk to a six-year-old about addiction? When he's two years old and reaches under the sink and pulls out the drain cleaner, we don't hesitate to tell him that the liquid in the bottle is a poison and could make him very sick. Tell him that addictive drugs can also make him very sick, that they are a poison to the system. Walking across the street without looking both ways is dangerous. If you get hit by a car, it could kill you. We take him to the street and point to the cars. We are not afraid to discuss the harmful effects of fast cars with our children. Don't be afraid to discuss the harmful effects of illegal drugs with your children.

If you see an article in the paper related to addiction that can be explained, bring it to the dinner table and talk about it. Explain what happened to the fourteen-year-old who was taken to the hospital after taking drugs. The most important point is to make the subject common table talk. Drugs are a fact of life for all our children and a threat to their future. They need to be familiar with the terms and must have open communication at home.

The following is a list of warning signs taken from a pamphlet titled *Parents: What You Can Do About Drug Abuse*, which is produced and distributed by the National Institute on Drug Abuse.

· If you find alcohol, drugs, or drug paraphernalia in your child's possession, there's a strong probability that your child is using drugs.

· Abrupt change in mood or attitude.

· Sudden decline in attendance or performance at work or school.

· Sudden resistance to discipline at home or school.

· Impaired relationship with family or friends.

· Ignoring curfews.

· Unusual flare-ups of temper.

· Increased borrowing of money from parents or friends; stealing from home, school, or employer.

· Heightened secrecy about actions and possessions.

· Associating with a new group of friends, especially with those who use drugs.

Although these behaviors may indicate drug use, they may also reflect normal teenage growing pains. By observing your child, getting to know his or her friends, and talking to your child about problems, including drugs and alcohol, you should be able to learn whether he or she is involved.

As a direct result of my work with children, I have been exposed to many cases of drug and alcohol addiction. Each circumstance is managed according to the needs of the child, and the appropriate professionals within the particular community are consulted and used to facilitate intervention. But my involvement in specific cases and treatment modalities is limited.

Harry L. didn't know or seem to care that I was not an expert when he called me at three o'clock on a cold winter morning. All Harry knew was that his thirteen-year-old son, Randy, was found by the police half frozen in a drunken stupor, and I was the only person he knew who worked with kids in trouble. I had been Randy's Little League baseball coach the summer before the desperate call.

Harry was at the hospital where his boy was being thawed and dried out. The chances were Randy would sleep through the next twelve hours, and as hard as I tried, I could not think of a reason to go there. I was tempted to say I would meet him in the morning, but Harry's pain and anxiety got me out of bed.

During the drive to the hospital, I thought about the Randy I knew and liked. The kids on the team were eleven- and twelve-year-olds. He was a better than average player, but the characteristic I remembered most was his sense of humor. Randy's gravelly, adult-sounding voice, freckled face, and sophisticated sense of humor created a charming combination. As I drove I started laughing as I remembered the time he slid home on a close play and was called out. Randy jumped to his feet with his hands on his hips, teeth clenched, and was glaring straight into the umpire's eyes. The crowd, most of whom agreed it was a bad call, quieted as they waited to see what this little kid staring up at the umpire was going to say. Gradually, the jaws relaxed and a toothy smile spread over his face as he said, "Sir, I think you blew this one, but I forgive you because you look like a decent man." His sense of timing was even better than the line, and everyone including the umpire burst out laughing.

He played hard and followed instructions without complaining. If someone had asked me to guess which boy on that team would have a problem with alcohol or drugs, Randy would have been one of the last on the list.

His parents, Harry and Marge, were nice people. They came to most of the games and were there when transportation or volunteer help was needed.

Harry was standing in the lobby smoking a cigarette when I walked in the door. He came across the room to shake my hand and tried to talk, but started crying before he could get the words out. After several minutes and two more cigarettes, I learned that Randy had gone to a party where the kids raided the parents' liquor cabinet. Most of the other children took only a few brave sips, but apparently Randy drank like an old trouper and walked out of the party. I asked Harry if this was a first for Randy, and he said he thought it was. I asked several other questions and concluded by saying that it sounded like an isolated incident, but that it might be a good idea to take his son to an alcoholism counselor within the next few days to get an opinion from an expert. Harry seemed relieved by my opinion, and promised to call and let me know how things came out. Randy was sleeping, Harry was quieted, and I went home.

The promised call came two years later. This time fifteen-year-old Randy was in juvenile detention. He had been picked up for stealing tires from a local merchant to feed a drug habit that was estimated to cost $300 a day. The robbery was his third felony in nine months. Harry called to tell me his son was a lost cause. He and Marge had agreed to put him out of their lives forever. Randy had hurt them for the last time. The probation officer said he would be sent to the reform school, and the family had concluded that he was now the state's problem. The very fact that Harry called me attested to the lack of conviction in his statement, but there was no doubt that he was running out of patience with his son and his son's addiction.

We agreed to meet for coffee. The story was not unlike many that I had heard before. After the first incident, Randy convinced his parents that the drinks at the party were his first and would be his last. There was no need to see a counselor. Several months passed before Marge noticed that Randy had lost his sense of humor. In fact, he was getting mean. Harry attributed it to adolescence, but felt uneasy. Randy's old friends were gone and the replacements were older, moody kids with "dirty hair and smart mouths."

While we were talking, Harry became reflective and

said that there were several times when he knew something was wrong with his son, but kept putting it out of his mind and hoping for the best.

When Randy was fourteen they found bits of marijuana in his desk drawer. They confronted him with the evidence, and he said it belonged to a friend he was trying to help. His parents believed him. A few months later, he was arrested for stealing money from the school office. When the police asked him why he needed the money, he said he owed it to a friend. The friend was his dealer. During the twenty-four-month period following the first discovered drink, Randy had written $1,400 worth of bad checks, all covered by his father, and stolen the family car twice.

I asked Harry if he knew what the term "enabler" meant. Harry said, "Those counselors we took our kid to had all kinds of catchphrases like that. We took him to three of those jerk experts, and none of them did any good."

Harry and Marge were classic enablers. They spent the first year and a half of his addiction denying he had a problem. They would call the school and say Randy was sick when he was hung over or staying at a friend's. They would promise the court and the police that they would get him help, but when Randy would beg them not to send him for inpatient care, and promise never to drink or take drugs again, they believed him. (It should be noted that all three outpatient counselors had recommended inpatient care.) They would pay fines. They negotiated with merchants from whom he had stolen goods. As far as Randy was concerned, Harry and Marge had a problem, he didn't.

For two years they enabled Randy to continue his addiction, and then decided that they would kick him out. I agreed with Harry that it was time for Randy to accept the consequences of his actions, but he didn't have to be disowned in the process. Addiction is a family problem. It affects everyone in the family, and when it comes time to deal with it the entire family has to get involved.

When confronting addiction, it is appropriate to take a hard-line approach. In essence you say, "We love you, son, but we can't pay your fines. You got them, you pay them. We can't bail you out when you refuse to accept the responsibility for your own problem. We won't pay your bad debts or your bad checks. We *will* pay for inpatient treatment, we *will* get involved in the treatment process, and we *will* follow the advice of the people who know what they are talking about."

This all sounds very logical until you see your child sitting in a drunk tank with fifteen hard cases. It is not easy, but with support from professionals who know what they are doing, addiction can be controlled.

By this time Harry was bordering on being a nonbeliever, but the glimmer of hope was still there when he asked what they should do now. We contacted a reputable treatment center, which agreed to have a representative visit Randy. The juvenile judge was cooperative and agreed to substitute treatment for commitment, but the reform school commitment would be reinstated if he refused to stay in the program.

Please note that I said we contacted a *reputable* treatment center. If you feel the need to see a counselor or send your child to an inpatient care facility, consult your local physician or someone in the mental health field you trust.

The next time I got a call, Harry said, "These damn treatment people want me to take a week off and go in to be a part of this thing called family week, and I told them that my good friend and expert, Kent Hayes, told me that the problem was Randy's, and I didn't have to get involved with his shit anymore." I laughed and told him he was the purest example of a selective listener I had ever known. He took the week off and came to my office immediately following his experience, bubbling over with information.

Family interaction was the third week of Randy's treatment, and the boy Harry and Marge saw resembled the kid who played baseball the summer he was twelve. He was bright, and he was funny. But the greatest breakthrough was his willingness to admit he was and is an alcoholic and a drug addict.

The week was tough on both Randy and his parents. They learned what they did wrong and had to face some hard facts about a disease that would not go away with some magic pill. They had to sit facing each other and talk about feelings in front of strangers. But they learned that these strangers had made the same mistakes they did. Harry learned that the angry, rejecting feelings that this dreadful disease had fostered were shared by others in the group.

The sixty-day treatment program was the beginning of a lifelong process. It wouldn't be easy, but for the first time the whole family knew it and knew what had to be done.

I called Harry before I wrote this to find out how his son was doing. Six months after his stay in the hospital, Randy had a relapse. He went to a football game and came home high on drugs. But this time Harry and Marge knew what to do. They called his contact person at AA who was at the house within ten minutes. Randy went back to the hospital for twelve days. Harry said that this time he didn't feel out of control or that the world was coming to an end. It was a relapse, and they had been warned that it might happen.

As far as they knew, Randy has not imbibed since that football game nine years ago. He is now married and has two children.

We also talked about those bad years, and the "what if's" that could have been devastating for all of them. When I told him I was writing this book, Harry said I had to tell parents to be bold and talk to their kids if they suspect they are taking drugs. I asked him how you bring up the subject without sounding accusatory or snoopy. He didn't know, but was sure I would find a way.

You start by telling your children you are going to ask some hard questions if you ever suspect they are experimenting with drugs. Open the subject before alcohol or drug abuse becomes a reality. Tell them that you would talk to them about cancer if they exhibited the symptoms, and that addiction can also be deadly.

Most children will experiment with some form of drug abuse. Parents who deny this likelihood will not be prepared to see the talltale signs. If drug usage is a familiar topic in your family, it will be easier for you to ask the hard questions.

If your child is heavily involved, the chances are good that their response to your questions will be volatile if not violent.

Every expert in the field will tell you that the sooner parents discover the problem and confront the issue, the greater their chance of successful treatment intervention. There is an ongoing debate as to whether alcohol and drug addiction are diseases. Although I feel no compulsion to choose sides, I do know that I have never known an addicted child or adult who did not use drugs or alcohol to compensate for or hide from other deep-seated emotional problems. People use mind-altering substances to create a state of happiness or comfort that they think cannot be achieved any other way. They say that the only time they are not homesick, sad, or in need of comfort is when they get high. I have heard addicted men say that the only time they felt like adequate males was while they were intoxicated. I have listened to teenage girls talk about being rejected by close friends. The only way they could tolerate their feelings of alienation was by obliterating the hurt with drugs.

Addictions can provide instant relief from pain. But this relief is only temporary. When we concentrate on the addiction and ignore the cause of the pain, we are fighting a losing battle. It can be extremely difficult to get someone to confront painful feelings while he is still using drugs, but it is also true that addiction maintains its power if the core hurt is not dealt with.

Nothing would give me greater pleasure than to be able to give all the loving mothers and fathers in this world a formula that would protect their children from addictive substances. I don't know that formula, but as I try to reconstruct the known and accepted preventive and treatment measures, I discover I am repeating the advice I have given throughout this book. Parents who provide a nurturing, structured environment and communicate with their child have the best chance of dealing with substance abuse.

13

Husbands and wives
who do not love each other
produce disturbed kids.

They all have the same disinfected smell. But this particular prison was old, and the rotting stone walls, combined with the smell of perspiration, gave this ugly Southern institution a pungent odor of its own. It was July, and the warden's office and the reception area were the only sections that were air-conditioned. I was there to consult with the warden and his staff and was scheduled for a tour of the prison.

No matter how many times I tour these institutions, I never get used to them. Most of what we cherish in life is taken away. Privacy, dignity, a sense of security, freedom, and most of your hope is checked in at the front door with your personal belongings. Guards patrol the catwalks and watch the outside walls, but everything down on the floor is run by prisoners. Many prisoners live with constant fear of being raped or killed. When you walk into their presence, you feel the anger.

One third of the institution was set aside for the inmates who were twenty-one and under. We had just entered this area when I heard my name spoken from one of the cells. I stopped the group and walked back. I recognized the face immediately, and my heart sank. My first thought was that one of the children who had graduated from one of our programs had screwed up.

There was a yellow line painted four feet in front of the cell doors. No one was supposed to step over this barrier. The policy was instituted after an incident in which prison personnel had their necks broken by angry prisoners. I knew the rule, but forgot it as I started to walk toward the blond, blue-eyed boy. He told me to stay back, and I was immediately offended. He saw my reaction, and apologized as he explained the rule. "You don't know who I am, do you?" I confessed my ignorance. When he told me his name I stood there too stunned to react, and not sure what to say next.

He was David C., a child who grew up across the street from my family when I was in high school. Throughout this book I have talked about the increased numbers of disturbed kids coming from upper- and middle-class homes, but each time it touches me personally, the dismay is authentic. I asked the treatment coordinator to have David taken to the visitors area and discontinued the tour.

David's parents were both respected, upstanding members of the community. They had two boys; David was the younger one. Even though I saw them practically every day, I didn't know them well. The parents were attractive, well dressed, and almost always together. They drove to and from work in the same car, and I would see them working in the yard on weekends.

Having David transferred to the visiting area was a major event, and it took time. By the time he got there, my curiosity had gone into overdrive.

Even in prison, you start a conversation with the same safe conversation openers. "How are you doing?" "It's been a long time." I think we ask these nonquestions, and expect nonanswers, to give us time to look each other over without having to think about what's being said. I looked hard, but there was nothing on the exterior that would provide a clue. David looked exactly as I would have expected him to look if I had seen him on the street at home. The handsome smile was just as charming, and the handshake just as firm.

He was in prison for robbing banks. He and two friends had held up four banks in two states. He was serving a five- to fifteen-year sentence in the state we were in, and was facing another sentence in another state when he was released. This part of the conversation was easy. He described the robberies and resulting trial in a casual monotone. I finally asked how he had gotten himself into this kind of mess. He shrugged and said he had run away from home when he was fifteen, and had been stealing since. I then asked why he ran from home. He looked at me for several seconds, and then asked me what I thought of his parents. I told him they looked like nice people, but that I didn't know them that well.

David then told me about his home life and how his parents loved their fights. They would fight over anything and then insist that the boys take sides. David and his brother would hide in various parts of the house and yard to avoid being brought into these ugly conflicts. His parents never fought in public, and the neighbors were never aware of these emotional fisticuffs, but the inside of that home was in continual turmoil. David said you could feel the hate. There were some good times, but it was just enough for him and his brother to see what life could be like in a caring household. David's older brother ran away at the age of fourteen.

Husbands and wives who do not love each other produce disturbed kids.

It is difficult to overstate the value of living in a household with loving parents. When affection, respect, and love are present in a marriage, the children are secure and happy. People can ignore practically all the other parenting issues and still end up with a dandy kid if they are truly committed to each other. I might add that I have never seen a happily married couple with a shortage of nurturance for their children. The children who witness these secure relationships are blessed and thrive, but those exposed to an environment of anger and hostility are caught in a trap from which it is impossible to escape.

Nothing is more beneficial to creative child rearing than a healthy marriage, and nothing is more detrimental than a troubled one. But few unions are perfect, and few are absolutely bad. The reality is that most of us fall somewhere in between, feeling terrific about our spouses one day and not so terrific the next.

We seldom think that improving and maintaining the relationship with one's mate is an essential ingredient in raising healthy children. Children feel secure when their parents are happy with each other. Children who feel secure seldom commit crimes or need to abuse others to meet their own needs.

Conversely, parents who do not have a healthy relationship create unspeakable problems for their children, the most destructive of which is the children's conviction that they are the cause of their parents' misery.

After seeing what I have this past twenty-five years, I believe that people who have made an honest attempt to reconcile their differences and fail should consider getting a divorce. Many couples who say that they want to preserve their marriage "for the kids' sake" are deceiving themselves. They are using their children as an excuse to cover other more selfish fears, concerns, and needs. Bad marriages often feed on themselves; the combatants begin to thrive on the conflict. The battle becomes so all-consuming that the couple does not stop swinging at each other long enough to realize that they are battering their children.

I have listened to these children as they describe the atmosphere at the dinner table when their parents refused to talk, and everyone present knew that the slightest provocation would cause a violent eruption of anger directed at those unlucky enough to be there. The parents are then shocked when their kids run away. I have held these children when they tell me it was their fault that their parents screamed profanities, slammed the doors, and spent days not talking to or looking at each other.

You are not doing your child any favors when you force her to share your nightmare.

Please be aware that I do not give this advice lightly. My three oldest children, their mother, and I have lived through a divorce, and know the pain associated with this gruesome process.

I am not saying that you should jump out of the contract the day you feel the blush has left your romantic rose. I am saying that people with children have an obligation to maintain a reasonably compatible relationship. If that is not possible with your mate, you need to evaluate the impact of your shared hostility on your child.

What is compatibility? Is it always being sweet to each other, never saying a harsh word? Of course not. All of us have our squabbles and healthy disagreements, but when differences of opinion turn into vindictive personal attacks, you have crossed a line. Your children are bound to be affected by the emotional climate.

We have all been told that it's good to express our feelings. If you feel something, show it. If you are hurt and angry, let the world know. The concept is sound, up to a point. We all need a time and place to vent our wrath, but the best place is not in front of the kids. It doesn't hurt for them to witness some situations in which the husband and wife have an argument and make up. They need to know that adults, and especially parents, can disagree without falling apart. But there is a big difference between a disagreement and a fight. In the former you take the opportunity to express your feelings, but in the latter the intent is to hurt and be destructive.

A certain amount of decorum and dignity is of value in a marriage. I may be sounding like a stuffy old Englishman, but I have seen too many children destroyed by uncontrolled parents. *Your compatibility is their security.*

Ironically, it was while I was trying to find the right words to express just how important marital compatibility is to the security of children that I had a fight with my wife, Ginger. Anyone who knows her will tell you that it is hard to have a fight with Ginger, but if you work at something, it will happen.

The situation was typical of couples trying to coordinate two jobs and care for the children. I had set up an appointment to have the car fixed late in the evening. Ginger is a nurse, and works at the local hospital when they are short of staff, usually about three days a week. While she is working, our son Nicholas goes to the home of a remarkable woman who takes care of several children. Like most kids, he resists at first but has a good time when he gets there. Gayle and her batch of kids are a good diversion for a child who needs to be around other children.

Ginger and I had agreed that when she got off work, she would pick up Nicholas and then me, and we would all take the car in together. I hate to take the car in. It seems to consume the whole day, and the notion of being able to complete a full day's work and still get the car fixed sounded great. But Ginger was an hour late. By the time she drove up the drive, I was furious. I jumped in the passenger seat and chewed her out. It didn't matter that there was a code blue and a patient was dying, I had this appointment, and she knew it. She calmly explained why she was late, and I said I was tired of taking care of the goddamned cars. If she wanted the stupid car worked on, take it in herself. Nicholas was sitting in his car seat, and hadn't said a word. I turned around. His face was white, and he said, "Hi, Daddy." He doesn't see many fights, and he was obviously affected by the hostility.

We went in the house and Ginger went upstairs to change clothes. She was gone longer than usual, and Nicholas asked several times about her absence. I muttered something that didn't seem to satisfy him, but eventually she came down. We hadn't planned anything for dinner, so I said I was going to pick up hamburgers. Nicholas wanted to go. We had just pulled out of the driveway when he said, "I want to go to Gayle's." I asked why he wanted to go to Gayle's. "Because my house is broke." My two-year-old son had just told me what he thought of my little outburst. I had expressed my anger, and I may have felt better for having gotten it off my chest, but it wasn't worth the pain it had caused.

When we got home I asked Nicholas to repeat what he had said in the car. He did and I thought Ginger was going to cry. We kissed and made up and Nicholas grinned.

If your house is broke and you can't seem to get it fixed, it is time to get help. There are experts on marriage. These marriage counselors have the skills to help you see what you are doing to each other and present options that most of us have never considered. They will talk about the patterns your fights take, and how to stop them from degenerating into personal attacks.

A professional marriage counselor can help us see that much of our anger is misdirected. The source may be found in stressful jobs, impossible schedules, or unconscious conflicts that have nothing whatsoever to do with the spouse we are yelling at.

Couples get into comfortable ruts. They may be destructive, or boring, but they are comfortable. We stay in these ruts because of our fear of change.

Some friends of ours described their situation before they sought help. Theirs was not a bad marriage, it was simply a dull one, and they had started to fight. Dale came home from work, put on the same pair of old pants, drank two beers, had dinner, and fell asleep in front of the TV by eight-thirty. Mabel would sit there looking at his open mouth, and his gut hanging over his pants, wondering how long she could be bored without going crazy. After two sessions, a counselor suggested they change their schedule. Mabel enrolled in an exercise program for three evenings a week, and Dale joined the local drama group. He had dreamed of acting for years, but had never said anything about it until he was encouraged by the marriage counselor to profess his hidden dreams.

Like everyone else they have schedule conflicts, but they are again in love. Dale has lost his gut, and Mabel feels like a million dollars. This may sound simplistic, and you may be thinking this fool doesn't know what a real marital problem is. But most problems between two people are not so terribly complicated, and a marriage counselor can be the catalyst for remarkable changes.

Children thrive in homes where their mothers and fathers love one another. Children are destroyed in homes where the only bond is a mutual hate and distrust.

If your house is broke, fix it.

Conclusion

There is a story about a man who decided he needed a new suit, but didn't have much money. He reluctantly went to a cut-rate clothier, and was surprised to find a suit that looked pretty good. A slick salesman fitted the suit and told him to come back the next day. When he tried the garment on, he realized that one sleeve was too long, the waist was too big, and one pant leg was shorter than the other. He complained to the salesman, who assured him that the discrepancies were minor. If he just lowered one shoulder, the sleeve would fall to his wrist. If he pushed out his stomach the waist would feel snug, and if he bent his left knee, the pant leg would look just like the right one. The man finally agreed and limped out of the store wearing his new suit. Two barbers sitting in their chairs saw him walk by. One turned to the other and said, "Do you know who that poor twisted man is?" The other said, "No, but his suit sure fits good."

If you try to do everything I have told you in this book, you will look like the man in the cheap suit. This is not a step-by-step, how-to book. It is one man's observations and conclusions after spending twenty-five years working with troubled kids and raising five children. Each of you has your own beliefs and if you do not incorporate that individual style into your interaction with your children, nothing will work. A young child is the most perceptive animal on earth. Parenting these sensitive creatures properly requires absolute honesty.

If you read this book and put it down believing there is no hope for you, or your child, then I have failed to get my point across. There are no perfect children, or parents.

Raising children is a high-risk business. There are no guarantees, and the best of parents will have problems, but the successful ones learn how to confront them. The others will continue to avoid their responsibilities.

If you are an average parent with two or three children, the odds are that one of the plagues of modern society will visit your home: emotional breakdowns, criminal behavior, chemical dependence, or eating disorders like anorexia nervosa or bulimia. Many of these newly prevalent obsessive-compulsive behaviors are a product of the drastic changes going on in our society. Many children with anorexia or bulimia believe they are trimming down as they attempt to comply with social standards of appearance, but in fact they are starving themselves to death. These new obsessive-compulsive behaviors are just one of many signs that we must think about the messages we give to our kids. We must adapt our parenting skills to modern society. Vast changes are affecting the family, but we haven't yet made the concomitant adjustments in this "sacred" institution. As we think about these changes and new perspectives, we cannot forget to rejuvenate and update our concepts of family.

In the majority of households both parents now work. In many cases the wife is the primary income producer. With the divorce rates on the rise, single parenting has become a fact of life in many homes. When we try to apply the old ways of parenting to these new circumstances, we fail and end up feeling guilty, impotent, and angry.

In this book I have tried to remind you of some of the specific responsibilities that need to be addressed if you hope to raise an emotionally healthy child. I have talked of such things as nurturing, structure, and positive attitudes. Regardless of how parents make their living in order to survive financially, children still have these needs.

It is difficult for youngsters to grow up when their parents are too preoccupied to parent. Psychiatrists and psychologists have come up with a new parent-child concern. Today's buzz word in mental health is "bonding." They say that children are not bonding with their parents.

The truth is that kids can't bond with a moving target. They can't become attached to someone who is not there, or is only occasionally there. Parents who are preoccupied with their jobs, themselves, or their problems are not available to their children.

You *can* work and also be a good parent. But you must first define the practical tasks that must be accomplished in order to satisfy your children's basic needs. You then need to put caring for your child on your emotional priority list. If family and home take a backseat in every situation, no book or professional can help you out.

If you look closely at what I have written, you will discover several inconsistencies. At one point I say you have to work as hard at parenting as you do at your job. In another section I tell you to relax and enjoy your kids. I talk of setting structures and in the same chapter tell you to be spontaneous. I stress the value of nurturing and of a loving marriage—both traditional parenting concepts that will never be replaced. And yet I speak of new concepts that replace the old.

Oscar Wilde said, "Consistency is the last refuge of the unimaginative." After this book I will never be accused of being unimaginative. It comes down to this: I have worked with children too long to place real value on rigidity. Anyone remotely involved with raising kids will tell you that you had better be capable of adjusting, or be prepared to be left in the dust.

Caring for children is one of the craziest, most exciting undertakings I know of. It's never the same, and the potential for adventure is unlimited.

Proper parenting is the heart of mental illness prevention. We are still at a primitive stage of understanding our own behavior. The new learning can take place in families, or mental institutions, or prisons. If it's all the same with everyone else, I would just as soon keep it in the family. We need to look at what works and what doesn't. We need to throw out the old wives' tales and bring on innovative thinking. The family is tough enough to withstand change, but it will become weak if ignored and treated like a fond memory.

When my daughter Lisa was young, I would put her to bed and tell stories about two made-up characters named Agabetha and Grenoble. She would not go to sleep until I told her an Agabetha and Grenoble story. These two imaginary little girls had some grand adventures, and there were times I would use them to make a point. If Lisa had a fight with a friend, Grenoble would fight with Agabetha and then they would make up and love each other again. When I wanted to tell Lisa what she should do if she ever got lost, I told about Agabetha and Grenoble taking a long walk and losing their way. After the story she would ask questions and would be interested in the topic. These two lovable characters gave me a way to lecture without being a bore. It was a clever device, but more importantly it was something shared between Lisa and me. No one else in the whole world has heard an Agabetha and Grenoble story, and no one ever will. It was ours, and will always be ours.

When Lisa reminded me of our bedtime stories I felt good. I thought to myself, "I am a good parent." I have always tried in my own bumbling way to do what was right for my children, but I am only human. When my children were small, I got diverted, was sometimes preoccupied, and was away from home too often, and the mistakes I made have taken their toll. But the one quality that allows me to be so presumptuous as to claim to be good is my tenacity. I never gave up on me or my kids.

Our world is too complicated for us to sidestep all the pitfalls. The problems will be there. Learn to cope, and when you hit one of those low points, do not waste valuable time berating yourself. Being summoned before the judge does not mean that you are a bad or incompetent parent; it only means that you and your children are human. Stay with your kid and resolve the issues.

With all of these responsibilities and potential conflicts, why be a parent?

We have babies and raise children because there is nothing on this earth that can match the excitement or joy of creating and caring for a child. There are moments when you see your child's first smile, or first step, or graduation ceremony, and a lump sticks in your throat, and your heart expands till you feel it will explode. They do not give Nobel prizes for parenting, but if it's done right, they should.

ABOUT THE AUTHOR

E. Kent Hayes is a national child advocate and juvenile criminologist whose experience working with deprived youth spans a period of more than twenty-five years. Hayes began his career in the criminal justice system as a probation officer and as superintendent of a reform school. He then joined the Menninger Clinic, located in Topeka, Kansas. In 1975 he co-founded the Menninger Youth Advocacy Project, an experimental program in which troubled children are placed in family-care homes run by highly trained adults. He is also coauthor of *Broken Promise* and *Find a Safe Place*, two novels based on the dramatic true stories of neglected children. He lives in Lawrence, Kansas.